The Hard Choice Habits

All achievement depends on the same
decision, the difficult one.

Blake Carleton

To my children Molly, Grace, and Caleb -
Thank you for being the world's best inspiration to make the HARD decision.

To my wife, Kristy –
I know most days I make it HARD to love me, so I am thankful you are committed to the principles in this book. You helped me push through my fears and turn this idea into a reality.

Table of Contents

INTRODUCTION

During the first six months of 2009, the importance of decision making consumed my life. As a leader in a $40 million-dollar organization, I spent the first half of 2009 dealing with what felt to be a constant stream of employee issues resulting from poor decisions. A staff person was rude to an important customer. A long-time employee threw away a promising career over falsified reports. A seemingly inconsequential dispute between two co-workers resulted in legal action. A male worker made inappropriate advances on a female colleague. Our organization lost out on a significant opportunity as a result of a poor presentation due to a lack of preparation. It seemed as if all of my time was consumed by situations directly resulting from poor decisions.

Simultaneously, I found out that I would become a father for the first time. My wife and I had been trying to conceive a child for over two years. We finally were successful as a result of invitro-fertilization. We knew early in the pregnancy that we were expecting twins to be born in December of 2009, and in June the doctors would be able to determine the gender of our two bundles of joy.

The big day arrived, and a mix of emotions flooded my senses upon learning that I would be the father of two *girls*. I was excited at the possibility of having two children who would always love me. I thought about them running up to me as I came home from work and yelling, "Daddy," and giving me a big hug. I then thought about two wardrobes, two ponies, two sets of braces, two proms, two cars, two college tuitions, and you get the point. As I tried to regain consciousness, I realized I had forgotten a significant life event, "two weddings." I wondered if I could require my daughters to get married on the same day. As I developed the talking points highlighting the advantages of a joint wedding day, my cheapskate emotions evolved into true concern. I found myself worried that my daughters might choose a jerk for a spouse or be in an abusive relationship. I quickly tried to move past the thoughts of these sweet little girls, eventually facing the reality of adulthood and having to accept the consequences of their own choices. I tried to get back to pigtails and pony rides, but the damage was done. I was officially scared to death have daughters.

The recent barrage of employee issues and the fear of raising two daughters underscored the importance of decision making. Decision making would be a skill that could carry my girls through any situation. The life skill of decision making has the most significant influence over ultimate life success, and I committed to finding a decision-making strategy that I could teach my daughters. The process by which people make decisions became my obsession. As I began to research decision-making models, I was surprised to discover the complexity of more academic decision-making models. Some examples of these models are Rational, Bounded Reality, Intuitive, and Creative. Each model has five or more steps and requires a high level of self-awareness. When decisions arose, these models rely upon a great deal of self-reflection and emotional maturity. From my perspective, the academic models exist in a vacuum. They underestimate the power of emotion, the impact of outside stimuli, and the pressure of time. Even as an adult, I didn't have the discipline or awareness to use these more structured, formulaic models. I needed a simple, teachable decision-making strategy that could be widely applied and easily put into use. For the next few years, I would read, study, and contemplate the development of a usable, real-world system that enables people to make better decisions in all aspects of their lives.

The culmination of my research resulted in a model I call, The Hard Choice Habits. Simple binary rules power my model. From my research, it became evident that many of the systems that direct our world rely on binary rules. Binary is defined as relating to, composed of, or involving two things. Many of our complex systems, when simplified is governed by laws that reduce down to option A or option B. Binary rules can be applied broadly, quickly, and offer a high level of certainty. For this reason, simple *binary rules* underpin The Hard Choice Habits. These habits enable people to make the best possible decision. For an action to become a habit, practice is required, and The Hard Choice Habits create a platform for practicing decisions in real-world scenarios. The Hard Choice Habits are based on four simple binary choices that can easily be practiced every day. The decider can use these simple, flexible rules in any situation. Every decision reduces to one of two options: an easy option or a hard option. The choice of EASY or HARD creates the foundation for the hard choice habits and is the foundational element of which the other three decision rules are built upon. Consciously or subconsciously, we all create our own unique set of rules that direct our decision making. The process of naming them in their most basic form allows us to practice our decisions throughout our everyday life. The practice creates a calloused mind that develops a layer of tough, resilient material enabling people to make wise decisions even when faced with the stress of difficult circumstances.

We make tens of thousands of decisions daily, and it is impossible to have one universal choice for the wide range of complex decisions we experience. However, when we reduce any decision down to its most basic nature, we find there are simple rules that can be applied to help navigate even the most complicated situation. The rules required to develop Hard Choice Habits are: HARD or EASY, TO or FOR, AND or BUT, FEAR or FORWARD.

As previously mentioned, the most basic of all the rules is HARD or EASY. By simplifying our decisions to HARD or EASY, we can practice making HARD decisions. Practice creates a work-out for the neurons that control your decision making, so the Hard Choice Habit framework allows a person to strengthen their metaphorical decision muscles.

The HARD choice is ultimately in the eye of the beholder. What is hard for one person may be easy for another. The Hard Choice Habit not only allows for the variation found in the thousands of decisions faced throughout our day, but the process allows for the unique attributes of each decision-maker. The Hard Choice Habits account for the genetic strengths and weaknesses of each decider.

The book is structured in four sections. The first section will explain why humans struggle to make good decisions, and how technology is only making things worse. We will then explore the necessary ingredients required to develop a functional system to support us in making better decisions. The third section explains the four decision rules that create the Hard Choice Habits. Finally, the last section will provide practical strategies to on how to implement the decision rules into daily life.

Wayne Dyer said, "Our lives are a sum total of the choices we have made." The goal of this work is to expand Mr. Dyer's statement. *A **successful** life is the sum total of the **HARD** choices we have made.* There is a proportional relationship between the total number of HARD choices a person makes and the ultimate level of personal accomplishment. The HARD choices are the payment required for fulfillment, happiness, and any form of success. **Achievement of any type correlates to the sum of hard choices a person makes**.

"If you learn to use it right, **the adversity**, it will buy you a ticket to a place you couldn't have gone any other way." -

Tony Bennett
University of Virginia Head Basketball Coach

SECTION ONE

THE TROUBLE WITH DECISIONS

The first step to solving any problem is admitting there is a problem to be solved. The harsh reality is that conscious and unconscious biases influence decisions made by all humans. Humans look for patterns and use heuristics to assist in the decision-making process. A heuristic is an approach to problem-solving that employs a practical method that is not guaranteed to be optimal, perfect, or rational. Simply stated, heuristics are mental short-cuts the brain uses to make decisions. These short-cuts save much-needed energy and critical amounts of time. These biases and heuristics significantly impact the rationality of our decision making. We think we are making rational decisions, but often we are basing our decision on systematic errors created from past experiences and/or current emotional states. These errors erode our decision-making capabilities. Stated simply, humans are not good at making rational decisions. This troubling reality is proven over and over again by brilliant behavioral economists like Daniel Kahneman, Richard Thaler, and Dan Ariely to name a few.

To consider a better decision-making process, we must first admit that the current one is ineffective. The good decisions you do make are more unconscious than conscious, making them more like lucky coincidence as opposed to intentional skill. We are not wired to make good decisions, but rather to survive and ensure the survival of species. The section of our brains that is the most recently evolved relies on a series of unconscious deceptions to re-enforce an internal message that humans are logical, smart, wise, stable, measured beings that are in complete control of our decision-making process. We tell ourselves that we are good at making decisions, and then we make poor decisions. Our brains struggle to process the stimuli from a modern world, and the rapid development of technology is making our ability to make decisions worse.

1

THE RIGHT WAY TO GO

"This fork in the road happens over a hundred times a day, and it's the choices that you make that will determine the shape of your life."

Liz Murray

As I started my journey to develop a reliable decision-making system, I was shocked to learn that the average person makes roughly 35,000 decisions per day. This estimates to about 2,000 decisions per hour and about two decisions every two seconds. The high volume of decisions seemed outrageous; however, as I began to research the different types of decisions humans make, the number became more realistic.

There are many more types of decisions than I

had initially considered. There are programmed, routine, operational, strategic, major, minor, individual, group, non-programmed, and personal. While there are hundreds of labels for a myriad of decisions, I did find that most choices can fit into one of three categories. Decisions can be reflexive, reactive, or strategic. We make a small number of reflexive decisions and a small number of strategic decisions, but a much higher number of reactive decisions.

A reflexive decision is simply one made on an impulse with very little conscious thought driving the actual choice. The fight or flight mechanism is an excellent example of a reflexive decision. The fight or flight reflex is generated from the autonomic nervous system, the same nervous system that controls fight or flight is also responsible for heart rate, digestion, respiratory rate, urination, and sexual arousal. In other words, reflexive decisions happen automatically.

Strategic decisions are exactly the opposite. Extreme time constraints do not pressure these decisions, and this large window of time gives a person the ability to examine multiple aspects of the decision. These types of decisions usually occur repeatedly and are most commonly linked to the business world. An example of a strategic decision would be deciding what product line to invest in, which marketing firm to select, what type of car to buy, whether to start a business or what kind of vacation should you go on this summer. In theory, organizations and people faced with strategic decisions have time to do research, and this removes some of the emotional pressure from the decision, resulting in the best possible choice.

A reactive decision is a decision made by an individual in response to outside influence. Outside influence is anything that we encounter that prompts us to choose one thing or the other. Examples of "outside influences" are things like alarm clocks, the dessert menu, and e-mail.

- Alarm Clock: Possibly, the most hated outside influence ever created. Your alarm clock goes off at 5:00 am as a reminder to go to the gym. Now you must react to the loud alarm and determine whether you get up or go back to sleep.
- Dessert Menu: You ordered the Cobb salad, drank only water, and you passed on the roll. You are crushing it on the healthiness scale. The dessert menu arrives, and you have an addiction to cheesecake. You are reacting to the menu.
- E-mail from an annoying co-worker: we all have that one colleague who just can't get it right. Your co-worker sent another inappropriate e-mail, and you have a great meme fired up that will be hilarious and publicly showcase their idiocy. The outside influence of this e-mail has brought you to another point of decision.

The first discovery on my journey to a better decision-making process was that our unconscious mind has a tremendous impact on our decisions. It became apparent that thousands of our decisions occur outside of our conscious mind. Scientists estimate that the human sensory system sends the brain 11 million bits of information per second, and our conscious minds can handle between 16 and 50 bits per second. When a group of researchers played French music in an English wine store, sales of French wine went up by 77%. In the same store, when German music was playing, sales of German wine went up by 73%. The researchers concluded that the sound of the music triggered an unconscious proclivity towards a wine that matched the music. In another study, researchers found that test subjects ate more food just because its container was larger. Moviegoers were given extremely stale popcorn. When this poorly tasting popcorn was placed in a larger container, participants ate close to 50% more popcorn. Did these big eaters enjoy the taste of stale popcorn? Of course not, but unconsciously the participants ate a certain level amount of popcorn as dictated by the size of the container, not the quality of the popcorn.

After wrapping my head around the three types of decisions, my mind wandered back to my daughters. I speculated that if I could create a simple set of rules, then I could provide them with a systemized way to make decisions. It would be these simple decision rules, practiced over and over, that would produce hard choice habits. The habit of choosing the harder option will serve as a foundation for their success by helping them make better decisions in all walks of life. I began to look for real-world examples of simple binary decision rules that improved outcomes. I was pleasantly surprised to discover UPS had developed that exact type of system.

Beginning in 2004, UPS did everything possible to stop turning left. The $50 billion delivery company systematically decided that when forced to choose between a left or a right, they would go right. UPS required drivers to take as many right-hand turns as possible. They developed proprietary routing software that removed every non-essential left turn. The new obsession with turning right didn't mean that UPS trucks never turn left. It just means that they chose to turn right as often as possible. Upon arriving at the actual "fork in the road," UPS goes right.

This strategy seemed crazy to me when I first heard about it. I couldn't believe that this would be a good thing. I pictured big brown trucks driving around in circles, making one right turn after another all day until they ran out of gas. (However, the company quickly proved that making a majority of right-hand turns had dramatic impacts on their bottom line.) Turning right significantly reduced the number of accidents UPS trucks experienced. (Research shows that 61% of crashes involve left-hand turns, opposed to 3.1% involving right-hand turns.) Yearly, turning right saves ten million gallons of fuel. Each year CO_2 emissions are reduced by 100,000 metric tons. Drivers travel six to eight fewer miles with each trip, by simply taking more rights.

All of this turning right proved to be cheaper, safer, and faster, all of which are excellent outcomes if you are a package delivery business. Some of the drivers were reluctant at first, but once UPS had collected the data, it was easy to demonstrate that choosing to turn right was a smart move. It almost sounds too far-fetched to be true, "when in doubt - turn right!" I imagine that the initial reaction to the "turn right" requirement was tough. However, due to the nature of their business, the intersection of the decision, left or right, was simple. It was not necessarily easy to make this transition, but the core decision of left or right is simple. What about a not-so-simple decision? What about a hard and complicated problem like the integration of public schools?

The integration of schools was a result of the unanimous 1954 decision in Brown v Board of Education. The Supreme Court ruled that public school segregation was unconstitutional. The lawyers for Brown argued that schools that were separated racially were unequal. Although this landmark decision was made in 1954, the challenge with school integration would be battled for thirty-five years, and even today, our society still struggles with the scars of racially segregated schools. The logical answer for school integration was to take black students and send them to white schools

Sending black students to white schools was a difficult task, but was it the best method to successfully integrate public schools? In many cases, the black students had no black adults to serve as an equalizing force towards the all-white establishment. Why was it determined that the best possible path would be to ask black children to overcome hundreds of years of discrimination - alone, with no adult support in an environment that viewed them as second class citizens? This path was taken because it was easier to direct black children into classrooms and, most likely impossible to integrate black teachers into the same all-white school staff structure.

Author Malcolm Glidewell dedicated an entire podcast to the idea that integration would have been more successful had we integrated both teachers and students. In his research, he found that many black parents in the 1950's were not concerned about the lack of education their children were receiving, i.e., the quality of the teacher. These parents saw their children receiving a better education than they had received. It was more about access than education -

access to closer schools, access to better-supplied schools.

The integration of black teachers would have been much more difficult, if not impossible. But in hindsight, it would have made more sense to facilitate both black students and black teachers into newly integrated schools. Can you see the challenge with this tactic? It is doubtful that teacher integration was even possible due to the social climate of the late 50's early 60's. Two things are proven true with the benefit of 60 years of hindsight. If society were to integrate teachers AND students it would have been more difficult, but it would have certainly been better for the black students.

Now, let's move on to the second statement - a strategic teacher integration plan would have been better for black students. How can anyone make that type of statement? Where is there any proof of that argument?

In the 2012 school year, the US Department of Education reported that of the estimated 3,850,100 teachers in the US 82% of them were white. Sixty years after integration we still have 8 out of 10 teachers represented by one race. Studies have proven that success in school is as much about role models as it is about instruction. Children will seek out role models that they can identify with, and the fastest most obvious way to identify with someone is through gender and race – the most visually obvious features of a person. We know that kids tend to aspire to be like people that they can see themselves being, which is why race matters. If that person looks like me, then that could be me.

It is the ability to relate that would have helped newly integrated black students perform better. Indiana University and Vanderbilt University completed a study showing that black students are three times more likely to be recommended for gifted services if they have black teachers. The researchers suggest that African-American teachers tended to offer a more positive view of black students' abilities, self-control, and other indicators of giftedness. A Johns Hopkins study has found that if a black student has just one black teacher in elementary school, they are significantly more likely to graduate. The uncomfortable reality is that if our schools had more black teachers, black pupils would have more relatable adult role models, thus making them more successful in schools. But painfully, integration of schools is not as simple as package delivery. UPS has the fortune to be confronted with a simple, binary decision at every turn – pun intended. The core of their business success at the simplest level is a binary choice of whether to turn left or right. Imagine if humans could reduce our decisions to the simplest form and then consistently make a right turn.

As I thought about my daughters, I felt confident that decision making was the one skill that could form the foundation of all other skills. No matter the skill, no matter the trait, the most important aspect of that character trait was the decision to act, the decision to choose a harder option over an easier one. I began to look for examples of people that had used simple rules to impact their own choices.

I have had the pleasure to see former President Bill Clinton speak. One of his stories serves as the first of many proof points in my quest to arm my girls with the necessary skills to be successful. During the first year of his presidency, his only daughter, Chelsea, was 12 years old. One night at dinner, Chelsea asked her father, "How are you able to deal with the constant criticism?" President Clinton reminded his daughter that throughout her entire life people would criticize her and that she had a choice; she could take that feedback *personally*, or you could take it *seriously*. He focused on the fact that no one could determine how you took feedback, but you. As I listened to Mr. Clinton, it was interesting to think about his mental process. He knew he would be criticized, often viciously and maliciously. He had decided that he would hear all that criticism, but he had already pre-determined that he would not let those words penetrate his confidence or his resolve. He would listen to them, but only at a logical level rather than the personal level. He had created a binary decision rule for himself. It was simple and could be applied quickly to a wide variety of situations.

Nick Saban, the head football coach for the University of Alabama, was being interviewed before his team played for their 8th National Championship Title. One line from his interview served as another proof point that successful people use simple rules to develop habits. Coach Saban said, "You don't practice until you get it right; you practice until you don't get it wrong." The mindset of practicing until you don't get it wrong is a much different mindset than practicing to get it right. Coach Saban chooses to mentally approach the outcomes differently and leads his team to have this same mindset. He had decided that in key situations when it was a matter of getting it right or not getting it wrong, he would push through the normal status quo of "getting it right" to his predetermined status quo of not getting it wrong. It was his scaled-down cheat sheet that helped him quickly push through the normal – "get it right and move on," to practice something repeatedly until – "we don't get it wrong."

I have come to know quite a few women how have admitted to me that they were sexually abused at some point in their childhood. Right or wrong, I have a habit of judging these women and placing them in one of two categories. The first category is women who, rightfully so, are defined by this experience. They have unhealthy relationships, they abuse drugs, and they struggle with life on a day to day basis. The second category is women who are successful, happy, and seem to have used the horrific experience to propel themselves forward. I spoke to a woman in this second category and was shocked at her resolve. I was curious to understand how she could take an event that could have been crippling to her and use it to make her stronger. The next five minutes were some of the most enlightening in my life.

This young woman went on to tell me that living with her abuse was the hardest thing she ever did. She struggled with it every day. And even though I saw a strong, confident woman - it was not always that way for her. The abuse did poison a few relationships along the way, and there were days when she wanted to let the past define her. She explained that every day she decides not to be a victim. She would tell herself, "I am not a victim. I am a noun, not an adjective. Suffering through my abuse only describes a brief time in my life; it does not make me what I am." Unconsciously, she used her own binary decision rules to create a habit. The simple rules were: noun or adjective, victim or victor, past or present. She told herself not to dwell on the past, not to hold on to the anger, and not allow herself to be defined by someone else's abusive nature. She admitted it was hard at first, but that over the days and months, she felt the daily decision not to be a victim was creating a sense of who she was. In time, her simple self-talk created a habit. She knew that if she could get past this situation, that she could conquer any situation.

As we concluded our conversation, she told me that her daily decision not to be a victim helped create immense inner strength. It was this ability to conquer the daily internal messaging not to be a victim that allowed her to feel that she could conquer anything. She believed her most difficult life experience had built the foundation for all her success. She was fierce, fearless, strong, confident, and the furthest thing from a victim. But she had to decide to be those things, which was not an easy journey. So, through her daily practice of deciding not to be a victim, she was able to rewire her brain to embrace hard things. She was comfortable in discomfort and obtained a level of resilience earned through the commitment to making the hard choice.

The more I get to be around extraordinary people, the more I realize their success is not just about talent, or that karma that has blessed them with an easier path and fewer hurdles. I have discovered it is quite the opposite. Whether you are a poor kid from Arkansas that becomes president, a football coach from Alabama, or an abuse victim, the common thread is a certain level of comfort in making hard decisions. The common factor of success is an ability to make hard decisions regularly so that making hard decisions becomes the default habit. It is the habit of choosing the hard option over the easy option that unlocks a person's potential, allowing them to be who they were created to be. Consider someone who grew up without parents, with no money, and every disadvantage you can think of. Despite these circumstances the person breaks the cycle and establishes themselves in a healthy, prosperous environment. Is that just luck? Is that simply a result of the odds working out for that person? Of course, the answer is no. If you look deeper into the background of this type of life change, you will find a person chose the hard path at key points in their own life. They didn't join the local gang, they decided to go and live with a friend, or they wake up early to do some extra-studying to get that "A" on a math test. Understanding and choosing the hard option is the key. It doesn't matter if you are a person who is born with unlimited opportunity and squanders it, or someone who is born with the deck stacked against you and come out on top. The ultimate reason for success can be reduced to the ability to make good decisions. It doesn't matter how each of us defines "success." Successful people separate themselves in their ability to choose the hard choice over the easier choice.

If decision making is the holy grail of success, then why then do we humans have such a hard time consistently making good decisions? What gets in the way of our ability to select the right option? Humans are made to survive, and in our modern world, survival and good decision making are not mutually exclusive. We have the misconception that the logical areas of our brain are in complete control and make sure we make the right decision. The truth is most of our decisions occur at the subconscious level, which means that the presiding goal is to remain alive. When you combine thousands of years of human evolution with the modern age of technology, you are experiencing a recipe for disaster.

2

THE PROBLEM WITH THE BRAIN

"She knew full well the enormity of her offense, but because her desires were stronger than the code she was breaking, she persisted in breaking it. She persisted, and her subsequent reaction is something that all of us have known at one time or another."

Atticus Finch, To Kill a Mockingbird

The problem with the brain is that it has evolved over thousands of years to do one thing - keep you alive. It has not evolved to make good decisions, because a "good" decision is very subjective, but alive or dead is pretty straight forward. The brain is wired to continually evaluate threats and then make sure that the entire body is out of harm's way in case the threat becomes a reality. To actively improve your decisions, you must accept the fact that you are wired to process incomplete snippets of information quickly. Your brain is unintentionally working to undermine the quality level of your decisions. As far as your brain is concerned, the priority is speed, not necessary long-term success.

In the struggle to navigate the threats of this world, the brain has evolved into the most powerful device on the planet. Humanity has yet to develop a computer that can process as quickly. The ability to think creatively, solve problems, show empathy, and do quantum physics is a testament to the power and prowess of the human brain. It is this brainpower that allows us to sit atop the food chain. Quick whits, powered by the human brain, enables our species to adapt to the environmental changes that might otherwise doom any other species. Our society, our culture, and our existence is a direct result of the power of our brain.

As powerful as our brain is, it is one of the key limiting factors in our pursuit of making better decisions. When presented with a choice, the human brain is woefully designed to make consistent, logical, beneficial decisions. The brain is a prisoner of the moment and primarily powered by emotion. The same hardwiring that allowed us to survive the plains of Africa is now limiting our long-term success by making short-term errors. We can't seem to get out of our way. It is our lack of decision making that traps us beneath a self-imposed glass ceiling. We live, but we fail to realize our full potential because our brain believes it is better to be good and alive, versus great and dead.

In 370 B.C., Plato created a rich metaphor to illustrate the struggle for humans to make decisions. During Plato's time, human consciousness derived from a person's "soul," not the physical structure of their brain. Plato beautifully articulated that the human soul consists of three parts. He described our minds as a charioteer pulled by two winged steeds. There was a white steed that represented good, pure, bold actions. The black steed represented an animalistic element that gets a man in trouble. The charioteer rounded out the third character in this description. Plato believed that the charioteer represented our self-consciousness, and the charioteer was in a constant struggle to control the opposing two wild steeds.

The technology revolution of the 20th century allowed scientists to stop hypothesizing about how the brain works by scanning the brain during the decision-making process. The scientific world quickly came to realize that Plato was not far off. Scientists now understand that the brain is composed of two complementary and competing mental systems. From my perspective, the best explanation of how humans make decisions was written by Daniel Kahneman in his groundbreaking book, *Thinking Fast, Thinking Slow.*

Dr. Kahneman proves time and time again that there is an existence of two minds housed in one physical brain. In his book, he calls the competing minds - System 1 and System 2. There are other metaphors used to describe the characteristics of each system. Dr. Richard Thaler and Dr. Cass Sunstein referred to System 1 as the Automatic System and System 2, the Reflective System. They further simplified the metaphor by naming System 1, the Doer, and System 2, the Planner. In his book, *The Happiness Hypothesis*, Jonathan Haidt, represented the two cognitive systems as the elephant and the rider. The elephant and the rider metaphor was made more famous by Dan and Chip Heath in their book, *Switch.*

<u>System 1</u> (the Doer, the Elephant): Unconscious, effortless, fast, associative, uncontrolled, and skilled

<u>System 2</u> (the Planner, the Rider): Self-Aware, difficult, slow, deductive, measured, and rule-following.

System 1 is a fast, automated, unruly system that runs on emotion with one job, keep you alive. It cares for nothing else and is wired to collect huge amounts of data from the world around you. To use the copious amount of information that is collected, the brain has developed shortcuts or heuristics. The shortcuts allow us to take action based on streams of fast-moving information from our surrounding environment. Without these mental shortcuts, we would be paralyzed by our desire to over-analyze the information at hand.

System 1 has created heuristics and biases to handle the influx of limitless amounts of information to make sense of a complex world. System 2, however, functions much differently. System 2 is deliberate, effortful, structured, logical, and thoughtful. System 2 is what each of us thinks of when we view ourselves as the rational, enlightened human brain. It is System 2 that has allowed for all of the amazing advances of the human species, but the limiting factor is that this system is lazy. Not only does System 2 not like to work, when it does work, but it also tires quickly. Unlike the fast, always working System 1, System 2 must be forced into action and would much rather just let System 1 do all the work. System 2 is always looking to conserve energy, so it takes quite a bit of prodding to get into the game. It is this air of lazy arrogance that underlies the main problem. While System 2 is technically in charge, it is weak, and does not have the agility, stamina, or processing power to keep up with System 1.

For me, the metaphor that makes the most sense in describing the daily mental power struggle is the

Elephant and the Rider. The elephant is System 1 - strong, powerful, easily distracted, unruly at times. The rider represents System 2 - logical, practical, calculated, and in control. But is the rider in control? The easy answer is yes - the rider can steer the elephant and direct the beast in the best direction to move. The elephant can and usually does accommodate the instructions of the rider, but what if the elephant decides he does not want to go right but wants to go left. Can the rider truly "make" the elephant go right? No, the elephant is the one in control, and the rider's ability to steer the animal is merely an illusion of control.

Even if the rider is strong enough to force his will upon the stubborn elephant, at some point, the rider will become tired. The rider lacks the power and stamina to control the elephant for any extended amount of time. There is a set amount of effort the rider can exert upon the elephant. The rider runs out of energy, and the elephant is left to trample anyone in its path. Parents experience this when they lose their temper at home after a long day. You have had to hold it together at work for the benefit of your paycheck, but once you arrive home, you don't have any effort left. You snap quickly over the most insignificant thing. In moments like these, the angry elephant of System 1 is stomping all of your loved ones. The official name of this occurrence is Ego Depletion.

Ego depletion is the idea that self-control or willpower (the rider) draws upon a limited pool of mental resources that can be used up. When the energy for mental activity is low, self-control is typically impaired. When your brain works hard, it becomes tired. One thousand years ago, if your brain became tired, you were much more likely to be unaware of your surroundings and get eaten by a lion. Survival requires that our attention observes the right threats, and for this reason, the brain looks to conserve energy until it is necessary to respond. Researcher Roy Baumeister conducted an experiment where he hoped to prove the existence of ego depletion. He started with two groups. Group one was forced to be in the presence of freshly baked chocolate chip cookies. The test subjects could smell and see the cookies, but they were not allowed to have a cookie. The second group of testers sat in a room with celery and radishes. Group two was also not allowed to have any celery or radishes. After 15 minutes, each group tried to complete a mentally challenging set of puzzles that was purposefully designed to force the students to quit. The outcome was that the "cookie" group gave up three times as fast as the radish group. The cookie group was using all their mental energy to not to eat cookies, so when they were asked to use similar mental energy on a different task, they didn't have the needed brainpower to complete the task. The rider was too tired.

The nervous system consumes more glucose than any other physical system in your body. Since we cannot guarantee when we will get the next "shot of glucose," the nervous system is always working to keep some reserve energy on supply. The impact of ego depletion was reported in the Proceedings of the National Academy of Sciences. A group of 8 judges spent the whole day reviewing inmates that were being considered for parole. The cases were presented randomly, and each judge spent less than 10 minutes on each case. The default decision is "rejection," and so the judges noted the exact time of their decision for each case. The judges reviewed the cases all day, with three food breaks allowed. Surprisingly, the researchers found that if a case was reviewed right after the meal, the judges granted parole 65% of the time. However, as time progressed towards the next food break, the parole outcomes changed significantly. The percentage of inmates given parole dropped to 30% right before the meal break. Our decisions are influenced by unconscious cues more than obvious environmental threats.

Researchers conducted a study in an office building where employees were on the "honor system" for their coffee. As they entered the coffee lounge, they were to deposit money into a jar for the coffee they consumed. A group of researchers developed two banners to hang in the lounge. The first set of banners displayed different kinds of flowers, but the second set of banners displayed sets of eyes. In the second set of banners, a single set of eyes seemed to peer down on the lounge. Some of the eyes looked happy, some looked friendly, while others looked angry or scared. The findings concluded that when the banners with the eyes were present, the employees put on average twice as much money into the jar. Researchers concluded that participants "felt someone watching them," but didn't even know it. In another experiment, researchers intermixed random pictures of eyes with visual noise (think the static image on your television) for 2/100 of a second. When pictures of dominant eyes were mixed into the images, the test subjects had elevated heart rates. These subjects did not see the eyes, but the mind subconsciously felt the eyes and pushed the body to react to a potential threat. Even though you aren't aware of it, you are always consuming stimuli and information from the world around you, and this information is impacting your decisions.

Humans are pattern seekers and use patterns to create a more coherent world. We make connections and patterns out of events that are not related. An excellent example of this is when shooters in basketball "get the hot hand." We see a player make ten shots in a row, and assume, "This guy is on fire, get him the ball. He can't miss." The reality is that these ten shots are simply a statistical outlier and that over time the player will regress to a typical mean shooting average. Because acts of terrorism are graphic and well covered by the media, we are inundated with images and information about terrorism. It is because of this front of mind characteristic of terrorism that people place "death by terrorism" in their top list of fears. However, there is only a 1 in 20,000,000 chance that a person dies from a terrorist attack. To offer context, a person's chance of dying in a car accident is 1 in 19,000, drowning in a bathtub 1 in 800,000, and being killed by lightning is 1 in 1,000,000. The irrational fear created by terrorist attacks illustrates how the human brain is conditioned to respond to what we see, making terrorism a real fear for people even if it is statistically very unlikely.

It isn't just what we see, but simple gestures can also influence our course of action. In 1988, Fritz Strack, a German social psychologist professor, authored an often-cited study proving the impact of simple gestures. This study asked a group of college students to hold a pencil in their mouths horizontally. Holding a pencil horizontally in your mouth causes the facial muscle to mimic a smile. The second group was asked to hold the pencil with the lead point to the ground with the eraser puckered in their mouth. When participants held the pencil in this manner, their mouth formed a frown. Each group was asked to read the same Far Side Comics and rate on how funny the cartoons were. The smiling pencil group found the same comic funnier than the frowning pencil group. These gestures seemed to be hardwired to the brain, impacting how we respond to the world around us. We think that we are deciding if something is funny or not, but without even knowing it, we are being directed by a host of outside stimuli to a specific level of humor.

Words we hear subconsciously impact our physical actions too. Psychologist John Bargh discovered the "Florida Effect." In his study, he asked students to assemble four-word sentences from a group of five words. For one group, half of the words were connected with older people - Florida, forgetful, bald, gray, wrinkle, etc. All test subjects were then asked to go from their current room to another room for another experiment. The group that read the words associated with older people walked from one place to the next significantly slower than the group that read random words. Exposure to words that connected to older people impacted the pace of the students' movement.

The evolved brain is lazy, irrational, and significantly influenced by emotion. The brain struggles to apply simple statistical principals regularly. The brain makes connections where there are none and looks to create patterns where there aren't any. The sensory messages that flood our senses manipulate our brains, and the brain misleads us by over-reacting to stimuli just because it is right in front of our face, not because of the factual accuracy of the stimuli. The brain has developed shortcuts to handle the onslaught of information to give us the best possible chance to pass along your genetic code.

The shortcuts were great while living on the plains of Africa, but now they cause us to make choices that are detrimental to our long term success. We are a top of the line laptop running on software from 1985 We have the hardware to keep up, but the operating system limits our ability. The influence of our antiquated software struggles to support good decisions in our current over-stimulated environment. A majority of the overstimulation we experience in our everyday lives results from the constant presence of technology.

3

THE INFLUENCE OF TECHNOLOGY

"I fear the day that technology will surpass our human interaction. The world will have a generation of idiots."

Albert Einstein

The irony of life is that with all positive progress comes unforeseen negative consequences. Nothing in this life produces only positive outcomes. There is always a flip side, a catch, a ying to the yang. I once heard a nutritionist say, "If it tastes good – spit it out – it is bad for you." My mother used to tell me, *"Nothing in life is free, but your mother's love."* All things come with a cost, even if at the onset you can't see the cost.

The human brain's strength is to consume information. The more information we can absorb from our environment, the better chance we have to survive. If the wind direction change, then maybe a storm was coming. A particular smell might predict an impending forest fire in the distance. More information is good, but we have limits to the amount of information we can retain and process. It has been the last 20 years where we have seen societies pushing those limits.

Technology is the application of scientific knowledge for practical purposes, and digital technology has experienced exponential growth over the last 100 years, which has produced more advances in technology than all of the other years combined.

In the evolutionary blink of an eye, humans have access to volumes of information through an addictive medium, the screen. The widespread proliferation of digital information has made humans addicted to the sights, sounds, and vibrations of their devices. Humans are addicted to technology. As the availability of technology has grown, so too has our dependence on that same technology.

- 1998 there were 9,800 daily Google Searches, and in 2019 there are 5.6 billion Google searches every day.
- 64% of Americans own a smartphone in 2016 - doubling from 2011.

- In 2008, people consumed three times as much information each DAY, compared to 1960.
- The average adult spends 20 hours a week on-line, which is double the amount from 10 years ago.

The extreme amount of exposure to technology is rewiring our brains. The bursts of information are playing to our primitive impulses. Our minds were designed to respond to threats and opportunities immediately. It was this response that kept us alive. The brain ensures that we monitor these rewards through the chemical, dopamine. When we respond to stimuli that we enjoy, we are rewarded with doses of dopamine. Once our brains have a shot of dopamine, we want another. We know that drugs, alcohol, and gambling addictions are primarily the result of our inability to resist the sensory pleasure produced by dopamine.

As the screens we watch rapidly change, the physical reaction allows our brains to focus on the incoming images, and this constant stream of visual stimuli shifts our orienting response into high gear. Anything with a screen can initiate the release of dopamine required for addiction to occur, so anytime we check our devices, the brain is rewarded with dopamine.

Simon Sinek made an interesting point about technology. He pointed out that "technology" is the only dopamine generator that is not currently regulated. Alcohol, gambling, drugs, all are addictive due to the dopamine that is produced, like technology. Mr. Sinek eloquently argued that as a society, we had accepted the cultural norm of handing over a dopamine-producing stimulate to a 12-year-old without any restrictions or government oversight.

We see that the allure of flashing screens and buzzing alarms stimulates dopamine and then creates a gentle addiction that results in a zombie-like state for all those that can't put down the device. The scientific community continues to gather research showing the consequences of this addiction.

- Studies have shown that glowing screens impact our ability to sleep. Now that many of us read on our cell phones or tablets, the bright lights are believed to confuse your internal light cues and sleep-induced hormones. Our eyes are especially sensitive to the blue lights given off by the screens, and these two visual stimuli impact our ability to fall asleep.
- Technology seems to impact our memories. A poll given to 3,000 people in 2007 showed that younger participants had more trouble remembering simple personal information. The respondents excused this by stating that they

have all this information on their phones, so why should they remember it.

- Studies have shown that the accessibility of calculators is decreasing simple math skills.
- A recent study conducted by Microsoft found that the human attention span has decreased 4 seconds since 2000, down to 8.25 seconds from 12 seconds. The study defined attention span as the amount of concentrated time on a task without becoming distracted.

The overwhelming availability of technology is making focus difficult, and the amount of mental distraction that surrounds our everyday lives is extensive. Primed by the current environment, it is the constant access to the stimulation provided by our technology that has given our brains a muscle memory for distraction. We no longer have to be trapped in our thoughts. We can lose ourselves in our Facebook feed, Instagram story, or merely checking the e-mail. We can dive headfirst into the rabbit hole and waste hours on endless articles, memes, and videos.

Technology seems to erode our impulse control. Impulse control is closely related to self-control. It is this trait that separates us from the rest of the animal kingdom. (Keep in mind that humans and chimps have 98% of the same DNA.) Impulse control allows us to stifle our short term "impulsive" actions to achieve long-term goals. By controlling our impulses, we can think long term and make plans. We can understand why a short term action might "feel" like the best thing, but be detrimental in the long run. The ability to control our impulses allows us to direct our attention and is a crucial aspect of long term success. As we relate this to technology, anyone who has ever texted while driving is showing a lack of impulse control. Every American adult that has a smartphone understands that there is no text worth wrecking one's car, but in 2011 it is estimated that 1.3 million accidents were caused by cell phone use. We feel or hear that text come in and we can't help but look, even though we know we shouldn't. Experts estimate people look at their mobile phones about 80 times per day.

The long-term problem that a shorter attention span creates involves our decision making. The decrease in impulse control directly erodes our ability to make good decisions. A shorter attention span and a lack of impulse control are the two forces that limit our ability to delay gratification. Researchers have discovered that delayed gratification is a good indicator of good decision making.

In its simplest form, delayed gratification is the ability for your system 2 (the rider) to regularly and effectively over-ride (control) your system 1 (the elephant). By delaying gratification, you are simply flexing your decision muscle. As the research has proven, it is one's ability to flex this muscle that can ultimately determine the levels of one's success. By delaying gratification, you are providing your "rider" with a form of training. It is very similar to a muscle. If you have strong lower back muscles, those muscles aren't just strong when you are picking up heavy objects. But the strength of these muscles will help improve your posture and support your entire back during other activities. It is the same for the strength of your rider (System 2). Research shows that one's ability to delay gratification is not limited to one area. If someone can delay gratification in one area, then most often they have the same ability in every area of their life.

The Marshmallow Test is considered the most famous research exploring delayed gratification. Dr. Walter Mischel and Dr. Ebbe Ebbesen were looking to understand when the control of delayed gratification developed in children. Groups of children entered a room, empty of distractions, where researchers placed a treat in front of them. The children could eat the treat, but they were forced to decide when to eat the treat. The premise of the test forced the children to either eat the treat right away or to wait 15 minutes and then be given a second treat. The initial results were that a small minority of test subjects dove in and just ate the treat as soon as they were left alone. By the end of the experiment, about one-third of the children were able to delay gratification enough to get the second treat. (These treats were usually marshmallow - hence the name "Marshmallow Test.")

The fascinating outcome of this study occurred decades later. In the first follow up study, the preschoolers who showed the ability to delay gratification were described to be more competent than their peers who did not show the ability to delay gratification. Additional studies showed that the preschoolers who could delay gratification had higher SAT scores, performed better in an academic setting, and had a higher mean income. The conclusion has been that these students demonstrated an ability to delay gratification, and as a result, these students made better choices. The skill of delaying gratification not only paid off when they were younger but seemed to help give these children the inside track into adulthood. The discipline to delay gratification positively impacted their ability to make better decisions. The key was that these "delayers" seemed to understand the long term value of delaying in other choice situations, such as studying or taking practice SAT exams. When researchers compared the "delayers" to the children who followed their first instinct and chose what "felt" the best at the moment, there was a noticeable difference in outcomes across many areas.

The explosion of digital technology has exposed the brain to a simple, efficient, addictive stimuli, the likes of which humans have never experienced. The visual exposure to these screens stimulates our dopamine centers and leads to addictive behaviors. The overwhelming amount of information made available by these devices has resulted in a shortened attention span and less impulse control. Attention span and impulse control are crucial ingredients in our ability to focus and make quality decisions. Thus, the digital environment we live in today is making an already difficult process of making decisions even more difficult.

SECTION TWO

THE FRAMEWORK OF A SOLUTION

Section one explained how the combination of the wiring of the human brain and the prevalence of technology impair our ability to make good decisions. If we are to push back on the forces that erode the quality level of our decision making, then we will need a system. Any successful solution must include three characteristics. The solution must be simple, fast, and adaptable. We do have examples of systems that use simple processes to tackle complex problems. The same characteristics that support the Hard Choice Habits are the same factors that power the invisible forces found in biology, technology, and spirituality. The best, most time tested systems leverage simple, fast solutions to produce optimum outcomes.

Consider the example below. Don't look down yet! Here is the test. See how long it takes you to count the dots in the box on the left. Then, track how long it takes you to count the dots inside the box on the right. GO.

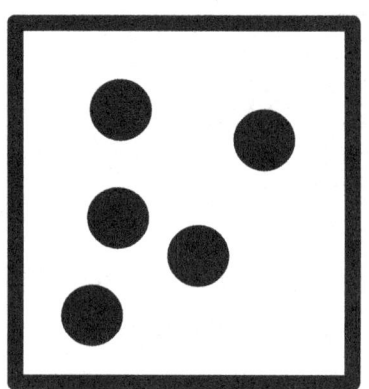 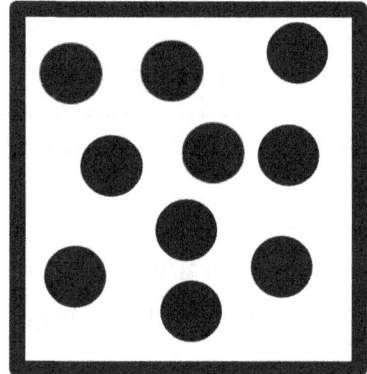

The average person takes about .2 seconds to count the dots inside the box on the left, and yet it takes a person about 1.5 seconds to count the dots in the box on the right. While there are only 100% more dots, it takes people 700% longer to count the box with more dots. The reason is that people SEE the dots as 5 in the box on the left, but they have to COUNT the ten dots on

52

the right. The counting takes brainpower, effort, focus. It slows down the process.

Fast and straightforward solutions are necessary because our brain is working so quickly that a slow, plodding, complex decision-making solution is impossible to use in the real world. The conscious mind (System 2) wants to use as little effort as possible and leave as much work as it can to the automatic System 1. If a decision-making solution requires a large amount of energy, the solution will never be used. A workable solution needs to be fast enough to slide in the conscious mind in conjunction with the thousands of other impulses flooding our brain.

Adaptability is necessary because of the wide range of non-linear decisions that will be faced daily. Successful systems need to be able to be used as often as possible, so if a system can only be used a handful of times throughout the day, it would not be sustainable. Repetition creates mastery, so the adaptability allows for higher usage rates, enabling the person to practice the system. Adaptability creates an environment for repetition, which ultimately facilitates a level of expertise that is not possible without practice. Any new system must be adaptable, and the good news is that the brain is as adaptable as it is powerful.

4

THE POWER OF THE MALLEABLE BRAIN

"The organ of thought is, within certain limits, malleable and perfectible by well-directed mental exercises." -

Ramon y Cajal – 19th-century neuroscientist

There was once a young woman named Ann who began to lose her sight at the age of 23 and became blind in her late thirties due to a spontaneous genetic mutation. Despite her blindness, she has been able to read a staggering number of books since losing her sight. Ann decided to use a computer program from Kurzweil Educational Systems that reads books to her aloud. This learning system helped her to increase the number of words read out-loud she understood, and after a gradual training process, she expanded the words she could understand to 340 per minute. Listening to 340 words per minute is quite a feat, and to a person with the use of all five senses understanding words at such a fast speed is almost impossible. Before losing her sight, Ann had an average reading pace. It is the loss of her sight that seemed to improve her auditory processing ability. This woman's brain, while losing some skills (the sense of sight), has compensated for that loss with a gain experienced in the pace at which she can understand spoken words.

Stephen Wiltshire is a British artist who can draw detailed sketches of landscapes after seeing them just once. Stephen was mute at a young age and diagnosed as autistic. At age seven, he became fascinated with the buildings around London. After briefly seeing images in books, he could create detailed drawings of the pictures he had only observed for a few minutes. Fast forward 30 years, Stephen is now famous worldwide and has drawn many of the world's major cities. To understand the scope of this work, consider his 2005 memory drawing of Tokyo. After a 20-minute helicopter ride, he spent the next seven days drawing a 32-foot depiction of what he had seen after only 20 minutes. The detail of his work might lead someone who sees his final picture to believe that they are looking at a photograph. Stephen's brain may struggle in social settings or to correctly read subtle facial cues, a common trait of persons with autism. But his brain has rewired itself to draw landscape scenes to perfection with only mere minutes of exposure to the landscape. The ability of the brain to rewire itself is not a genetic mutation occurring in a few select individuals.

It is not just physical challenges that cause a person's brain to reorganize itself. Scientists have found environment stimuli also prompt the brain to reallocate neural resources. The Sea Gypsies serve as an example of people who have had their brains rewired due to the realities of the environment they inhabit. This group of nomadic people that live off the West Coast of Thailand have developed extraordinary abilities. Sea Gypsie children swim before they walk. People of this culture can free dive at depths of up to 75 feet and can stay submerged for twice as long as an average person. The most interesting ability the Sea Gypsies have developed is their ability to see clearly in great depths of water. These people have developed the ability to control the shape of their pupils, and through this controlled mechanism, they can see very clearly underwater. The skills developed by the Sea Gypsies unique environment have allowed these people to flourish. Without the rewiring of the brain, the longevity of the Sea Gypsies would have at best been questionable, and more than likely, an impossibility.

The previous examples support the theory that the brain will reorganize itself to improve the chances of survival. Neuroplasticity (called brain plasticity or neural plasticity) is a broad term that describes the brain's ability to change. Up until the last decades, the scientific community believed brain development occurred only in particular periods and after these periods of time had passed, the brain could no longer change. This outdated philosophy assumes that if damage occurred during these critical periods, the brain was doomed to be defined by its current state, never able to improve. For hundreds of years, the world's leading scientists believed in this fixed brain theory. It was a forgone conclusion that once damage occurred that the brain was "fixed" or "static," so the experts believed that the brain could not substantially change.

The improvement in brain scanning technologies now proves that the brain is malleable. Beginning in the 1960's scientists began mapping the neural pathways within the brain. For the first time, a scientist could observe which areas of neurons within the brain became active during specific activities. As technology advanced, the neural activity could be observed with more accuracy, thus allowing scientists to have precise maps of the neural activity in the brain.

We understand that the brain wants to be as efficient as possible, which often is the cause for poor decisions based upon the shortcuts our brain creates - heuristics. However, in the brain's effort to be efficient, it engages the intricate neural pathways to overtake unused areas of the brain. Neurons don't "die" or get broken like other cells. If a neuron is no longer receiving stimuli, the brain uses these unused pathways to bolster the overall performance of the entire neural network. The brain realizes there are available resources and moves to take full advantage of those untapped neural resources. Our brains, just like other systems in our body, is a "use it or lose it" type of system. If the absence of stimuli persists, those neural maps may be used by other, more stimulated neurons.

It isn't just in chemical levels that we see the benefit of neurons firing together wiring together but in the physical structure of the brain. In 1962, Mark Rosenzweig discovered that mental training of animals increased the weight of their brains by 5%, and in 1973 researchers found that trained neurons develop 25% more branches than untrained neurons. When neurons are stimulated to fire together, this type of neural excitement results in a physical change that impacts the size, shape, and structure of the brain.

Once scientists discovered neural expansion in animals, the logical question to be answered was, did this same type of development occur in the human brain when stimulated? Researchers studied the brains of deceased people who were "educated" versus brains of "non-educated" people. ("Educated" was based upon the number of years of formal education a person had and were placed in three groups: 4-7 years, 8-11 years, and greater than 12 years.) The human brain had reacted very similarly to the animal brain once you expose your brain to stimuli, i.e., education. Educated brains saw increased branches among neurons, which caused these neurons to be driven further apart, leading to an increase in volume and thickness of the brain. By challenging the brain to make more neural connections through education, the educated person had unknowingly facilitated physical changes to their brain. These additional branches of neurons allowed for educated people to think faster than non-educated people.

In 2011, Eleanor Maguire, a neuroscientist at University College London, released one of the most compelling studies proving brain plasticity. Dr. Maguire studied the difference in the brain structure between London taxi cab drivers and London bus drivers. The streets of London are confusing. The street system of London is considered one of the worst street system in the world. The major roads sit at odd angles, and many of the side streets have dramatic curves. There are a large number of one-way streets and turnabouts. If you can navigate the streets of London - you can navigate anywhere.

Dr. Maguire was curious about how the challenging stimuli of the streets of London might change the brain networks of cab drivers. To mark this change, she would need to compare the brains of cab drivers to another group of people. For this "other group," she chose bus drivers of London. On the surface, these two professions do a similar job - drive people from point A to point B in the city of London, but these two jobs were very different in execution. The bus driver goes from spot A to spot B with little adjustment in route. Driving a bus in London is no different than driving a bus in any other city. You go from stop to stop - same path every day. However, cab drivers in London are always going to unknown places. They develop a new course each time they pick up a new passenger. Cab drivers never know where they are headed, so every new trip causes these drivers to account for a multitude of unforeseen factors: traffic, weather conditions, construction, and time of day. Said, in another way, cab drivers worked their mental muscles daily while bus drivers simply executed their routes on autopilot. Cab drivers in London are like well-trained athletes, and bus drivers are like couch potatoes just following what feels best and never having to exert much energy to accomplish outcomes of any significance.

Dr. Maguire looked at the hippocampus to see how the brain may be impacted by driving a taxi versus driving a bus. The hippocampus is the part of the brain involved in the development of memories. This part of the brain is also engaged by spatial navigation and remembering the location of things in space. After further research, Dr. Maguire found that the posterior hippocampus was larger in taxi drivers than bus drivers. The daily navigation skills enlisted by taxi drivers had caused their posterior hippocampus to become larger. Dr. Maguire could prove that the years spent mastering the streets of London had enlarged the part of the brain that was responsible for the successful navigation of the streets of London. Cab drivers flex their navigational mental muscle every day, and this mental exercise allows the cab drivers to "bulk up" their posterior hippocampi, like a weight lifter bulks up his physique through repetitive weight lifting. The cab drivers had performed rep after rep of mental weight lifting by navigating the confusing streets of London. These repeated "reps" helped to create a layering effect. With each trip, each new decision, each evaluation of outside influences, the brain was forced to expand the neural map responsible for successfully navigating the streets of London. Taxicab drivers that confront difficult driving become better at driving. Hard driving correlates to better drivers.

Physical stimulation, in conjunction with mental stimulation, like driving a cab in London, can greatly improve the connectivity of neural pathways and allow you to perform your desired activity better. Physical stimuli, paired with mental stimuli, is the preferred combination to increase neural connectivity. But the brain is so powerful that neural connections can grow without the reinforcement of accompanying physical stimuli. Researchers have recently discovered that neural connections can expand through thought alone. Your brain doesn't require the inclusion of simultaneous physical stimuli to rewire the neural pathways of the brain - the brain is powerful enough to provide the stimuli itself. A person can "re-think" their neural connections.

One of the problems with rehabilitating a severe injury is that to begin the rehabilitation process many patients must overcome intense levels of pain. On rare occasions, the pain of the rehab is so daunting that the patients cannot perform the necessary movements to rehab their bodies. An Australian scientist, GL Moseley, had an idea of how the plasticity of the brain may be able to help patients that experienced too much pain to begin rehabilitation.

Dr. Moseley asked patients to imagine they were moving their damaged body parts. He told them not to move, but to use their mind's eye to imagine in as much detail as possible the process of moving the damaged limb. Dr. Moseley asked these patients to look at pictures of healthy limbs in different positions. He asked these patients to imagine their limbs moving for 15 minutes three times per day. After some time, he incorporated these mental exercises with other more traditional rehabilitation techniques. To his surprise, twelve weeks later many of these patients reported that the pain diminished by as much as 50%. This feat of rehabilitation was remarkable. Dr. Moseley had created an entire treatment with no medication or invasive procedures - the brain had restructured itself to heal affected limbs.

The brain is an untapped power source in our pursuit of better decisions, but we must train our brains. The first step in making better decisions is believing you can make better decisions. You control the success of your decisions. You are not limited by your genetic code or by your environment. At the cellar level, your brain can rewire itself. People are not pre-disposed to make better decisions. It is a skill that is built up with practice and repetition. Humans can purposely rewire their brains to accomplish amazing things, including developing the ability to make better decisions.

By focusing on making better decisions, the neurons in your brain are exposed to a form of practice. The repetition of focused effort on purposely making better decisions causes the brain maps involved in deciding to be more precise. With an increase in accuracy, the neurons can fire faster. Once these neurons become faster, they begin to work more efficiently together. Your brain is ready to be rewired, but it takes practice.

All decisions have unknown variables that are unpredictable until the moment of the decision. Often these choices are incredibly complex. To make matters worse, the human making the decision is complex as well. The human decider is dealing with relationships, memories, fears, and countless other influences. As human beings, we must take into account the mental state of mind and the minute-to-minute level of our emotional state. It is valid to wonder if decision making can be practiced when the person is unaware of the exact moment of opportunity and that the variables of each decision are ever-changing.

Under our current construct of decision making, it is impossible to practice making decisions. However, by reducing decisions into broad groups of well-defined choices, we have a chance to practice making decisions. This reduced model is necessary for the development of a more systematic approach to decision making. Instead of having a wide range of options for every decision to be made, you must apply the simple rules to create a core group of decisions. (Example – UPS decided when faced with left or right, turn right.) The simplicity of these core choices allows for a host of decisions to be made consistently over and over again, which is the exact functionality needed to rewire the brain. By simplifying our decisions, we make better decisions. In the world of decision making, complexity abounds, but simplicity acts as a balancing coefficient in the equation of our pursuit to make better decisions.

5

THE ADVANTAGE OF SIMPLE

"Teacher, which is the greatest commandment in the
Law? Jesus replied: "Love the Lord your God with all
your heart and with all your soul and with all your
mind. This is the first and greatest commandment. And
the second is like it: Love your neighbor as yourself.
All of the Law and the Prophets hang on these two
commandments."

Matthew 22: 36-40

Christianity is the religion of choice for 31% of
the world's population. Scholars estimate that 2.4
billion people practice Christianity, and it is by far the
largest world religion by volume. It is incredible to me
that Christianity has gained such traction in 2,000 years

through a marketing plan that consisted of 12 uneducated guys, "spreading the word" on foot.

Jesus and his followers were Jewish. Most biblical scholars agree that there are 613 Jewish Laws established in the Old Testament. Of those 613, two-hundred and forty-eight are considered "Do Laws" and three hundred and sixty-five, are considered "Don't Laws." The scripture quoted from the book of Matthew describes a religious scholar of the time pressing Jesus to answer a pretty understandable question: of all these 613 laws, which are the most important ones. A regular person would struggle to remember 613 laws, and with such a robust list, it would make sense the laws could be arranged in order of importance. It could feel very defeating if all of the "laws" were regarded with the same level of importance. Abiding by 613 laws is impossible, so one might argue, why try.

Jesus was able to provide a much-needed dose of reduction to the 613 laws. Notice he doesn't say, "Don't worry about the other ones." He doesn't eliminate any of the Jewish law, but he provides followers with two simple concepts in which people can understand. Jesus reduces the elaborate list of laws by saying that all the laws "hinge" on two. He reduces the complex to the simple.

It is no surprise that Christianity spread so quickly; even if you don't agree with the religious principles of Christianity, you have to give some credit to the "stickiness" of the message. The advantage of early Christianity was that Jesus reduced the barrier to entry. A simple, straight forward rule book made it much easier to relate to the wide range of day-to-day situations in human existence. The simplification wasn't a specific do or don't list to every possible situation. It was rules-based. Christianity creates an instructional direction that can be consistently applied to a wide range of situations. By reducing the laws from 613 into a grouping of 2, it allows for both teachers and followers to stay focused and not get hung up in rule adherence. Jesus has effectively given his followers a "quick guide" to use as they move through a complicated world. We know that the brain has limited amounts of energy. If a person is trying to mentally navigate a complicated situation with complicated rules, they are defeated before they even start because of the energy drain of the entire process. The power of Christianity revolves around its simplicity to be applied to every possible situation.

Simple is so powerful because it has four characteristics that build upon one another, thus making it a requirement in any scalable process.

1. LESS EFFORT. Simple tasks require less effort. They have limited steps, processes, or procedures. Simple things are straight forward and leave little room for doubt. Because

"simple" has limited processes, it can be done much faster.

2. FAST.   Simple tasks can be executed faster. Fast tasks can be applied to a wide range of situations. I am reminded of the old adage, "You can always make a fast horse slow, but you can never make a slow horse fast." Fast is always good.

3. BROAD.   Simple tactics are functional across a wide range of activities, without dramatic adjustment. Simplicity provides a consistent structure that is transferable from one situation to the next.

4. REPEATABLE.   The flexibility allows for simple to be practiced over and over again. Simplicity allows you to focus on the few key steps as opposed to trying to remember a long list of instructions. The repetition engages the brain in such a way forms habits. Doing a simple task over and over again creates a level of automation, and it is this automation that forms the basis of a habit.

Humans have been struggling with simplicity since the dawn of time, and the recent advances in technology only make the problem of simplicity more difficult. Aesop's fable of the Fox and the Cat is the ancient story that addresses the difference between a simple, automatic action and a complex, multi-stepped effort. The fable tells the story of a conversation between a fox and a cat. The two creatures are discussing the ways each of them uses to avoid hunters. The fox brags of having multiple tactics to elude the hunter, while the cat confesses to having one tactic - climbing a tree. As the two animals are in this conversation, a hunter approaches, and the fox is easily caught because he is trying to decide which trick to use to avoid the hunter, the cat automatically does the one thing the animal knows to do, climb. The fox is caught, the cat escapes. In situations with multiple variables, simple outperforms complex.

Aesop might have used animals in this fable because simplicity abounds in the natural world. The natural world illustrates time and time again that simple processes can produce success in complex, uncertain situations. Take starlings for an example. Starlings in flight are known as a murmuration, and in the murmuration, hundreds and thousands of starlings fly in such a close formation that the group looks like a flowing cloud of smoke. This beautiful phenomenon seems so precise that while watching the birds in flight, one might insist that the entire event is choreographed.

Early scientists hypothesized that the existence of such a coordinated aerial display must come about in one of two ways. Either there was one "lead" starling who predicated the flight path and all the other birds followed suit, or that the birds were synchronized because of "thought-transference." The reason for the excellent coordination had to be that the birds had telepathic powers.

As science advanced, the "telepathic bird" theory was discarded. While early scientists could not understand how large groups of animals could coordinate such a chaotic event, a software engineer could. Craig Reynolds, a student at MIT, was in the process of designing computer graphic programs and became interested in digitally recreating the murmuration. While trying to reproduce this type of flight, he coded three simple rules to recreate the murmuration. The first rule is to avoid a collision. The second rule, head in the same direction as your nearest neighbor. Finally, stay close to your nearest neighbor. Digitally these three rules worked to help Craig create a murmuration on his computer. After behavioral biologists tested Craig's rules in the wild, they found that these simple rules could explain this type of collective behavior in a wide range of settings. The researchers concluded that these rules could dictate mosquitofish shoal, starling flocks, and even tell how pedestrians self-organize into lines in the street.

Crickets are another animal that relies on simple rules. The female cricket is not a picky gal. Her needs are pretty simple, and the way to get invited back to her place requires you can chirp three times per second. If you are the first guy to cross her path, that can chirp three times per second, score. Females have a simple rule - hear three chirps per second - mate. The next rule of cricket mating is even better for the less endowed chirpers. Rule two for the female cricket is to lower your standards. Researchers discovered that if after 24 hours a female cricket has not come in contact with a 3 per second chirping male, then Ms. Cricket settles for the less robust chirper and mates. These two simple rules make sure that the species can survive.

How can simplicity be so effective in situations that have high volumes of "unknown" variables? Human beings love to try to solve complex problems with complex solutions. In theory, complex solutions "address" the long list of challenges created by complex problems, but in real life, the execution of a complex resolution cannot be sustained over long periods. When faced with complex problems, we must fight the temptation of solving complex problems with complex solutions. It is a better option to work to simplify the solution. Stephen Lubby realized first hand that he and his team lacked the resources to develop complex, expensive solutions to solve one of the world's most complex problems, health care in the slums of Karachi.

The slums of Karachi, Pakistan, contain 4 million people living in some of the most crowed, deplorable conditions in the world. Sewage runs in the street, most of the water supplies are contaminated, and food shortages are normal. One in ten children dies before age five from diarrhea or breathing conditions caused by a lack of general hygiene. Stephen and his team were researching ways to improve the health of the people living in these slums. Making the problem more complex was political corruption, cultural challenges, educational voids, and broken economic structures. The amount and degree of the challenges facing the inhabitants of the slums seemed too big to tackle. Even the most helpful organizations struggled to know where to start.

Stephen and his team had a simple idea, get people to wash their hands with soap to see how that simple change might impact overall health. The critics argued that this was like throwing a pebble at a tank, but Stephen was undaunted and proceeded with this experiment. He gave select neighborhoods soap. His team provided a brief training and then left soap with each family. Upon returning a few weeks later, to his amazement, he found some startling results. In the neighborhoods that used the soap, he discovered 52% fewer children had diarrhea, 48% fewer had pneumonia, and 35% fewer cases of impetigo. It wasn't just "soap" that made this possible, but the soap ignited an activation phenomenon.

The activation phenomenon occurs when people experience a prompt in a process or situation and then feel a sense of purposeful participation in the task at hand. The activation phenomenon creates a focused sense of awareness on the momentary item at hand. Many families reported going from never washing their hands to washing their hands 3 - 5 times per day, and that the timing of these handwashing episodes was critical. They would wash before meals and times when they were exposed to a high number of germs. Using soap met all the qualifications of simple: easy, fast, broad, and highly repeatable leading to the unconscious use of soap. The soap prompted a behavior change that created significant impacts on the overall health of the participants.

Now imagine that Dr. Lubby and his team didn't give the people soap, but gave them all of the supplies to make soap. Would the outcomes have been as positive? Probably not. Because making soap is complicated and makes washing your hands effortful. The chances of this type of behavior change becoming a habit are slim, making soap is not simple, especially for people living in the slums of Karachi.

The power of "simple" is not reserved for the physical world of cricket mating, religion, and the Karachi slums. Our thoughts can be manipulated (for better or worse) through simple cues that create a powerful activation phenomenon.

The power of simple activation strategies is proven time and time again in studies researching heuristics and biases. In a study conducted by Norbert

Schwarz and his colleagues, researchers were able to show that when participants were prompted with the statement "Think like a statistician," they increased the use of basic statistical rules in making decisions. The statement "Think like a statistician" created a mental spark that activated the part of the brain that prompted the participants to utilize known higher statistical functions. It wasn't that the statement somehow caused more statistics to be known, but the statement activated the purposeful reliance on statistical rules. When another group of participants was prompted with the statement - "Think like a clinician," the opposite occurred - they used little to no basic statistical rules. By not using the basic statistical rules, this group performed worse. It wasn't that the "clinical" group was less smart or had less access to basic statistical information; the fact was they had not purposefully activated the areas of their brain to use statistical rules.

Simple processes that make an activation phenomenon occur at a neural level were more recently proven by a study conducted at Stanford. Groups of students were asked to solve a fictitious incident involving a food-poisoning event happening at a local eating establishment. Each group was given one of the three simple instructions before diving into the case study. The groups were given one of the following guidelines: (1) Listen to others. (2) Share your information. (3) Watch your time. After each group performed the exercise, the groups that performed the best were the ones that had received the instructions to "Listen to others." The worst performing groups were the "Share your information" groups. In reviewing the group sessions, the "share your information" groups talked over each other and spent a significant amount of time talking. None of these group members felt that they were consciously talking too much. From their perspective, they were following the simple prompt, "Share your information."

Whether a flock of birds, a health crisis, or solving problems as a group, a simple decision-making rule is required. A simple rule can be activated quickly and competes with the pace of your automatic firing System 1. Simple also helps to conserve the valuable brainpower required to take an idea from concept (thought) to reality (action). At some point in every reflexive decision, you will have to get System 2 involved. A simple decision-making tool allows System 2 to save the necessary mental effort to focus on the action, not on the decision. A set of simple decision rules will move your decision-making process from "deciding" to "applying."

A stewardess was walking the aisle and asked a gentleman in first class if he would care for a meal. The gentleman politely asked, "What are my choices?". The stewardess politely responded with a sly smile, "Your choice is yes or no." The simplest of all choices are binary. If a person is aiming for simple, a great place to begin is with binary.

6

THE REACH OF BINARY

"Try not. Do or do not. There is no try."

Yoda

  My family was blessed that my younger brother, Skip, decided one cold January day in 1998 to "do" and not "to try." His quick actions helped to save the entire family from years of heartache and sadness.

  I was a junior in college, and my brother was a senior in high school. As this type of story goes, my brother was out and about one evening and got into some trouble. This wasn't the typical "missing curfew" trouble - oh no, the trouble involved high speeds, alcohol, police, misdemeanor robbery, and lying straight-faced to my parents. It was by far the most significant trouble any one of the three children had been in, quite the bragging right for my younger brother. The following morning, after the dust settled, the punishment was passed out. My lovely brother lost pretty much any privilege he had for two months. He would go to school, basketball practice, and that's it. No phone. No dates. No leaving the house. Now, my parents weren't big "grounders" so the 8-week sentence was a never before seen occurrence in the Carleton home. It was such a harsh penalty that even my brother's nemesis - our sister (who was the baby of the family) felt sympathetic to my brother's sentence.

After the punishment was delivered, my father looked at my brother and said, "Your mother and I are so hurt, mad, sad, and disappointed that we have got to get out of this house, and since you can't leave we are heading to lunch and a movie. We will be back for dinner, and if you are lucky, we will allow you to eat. I have just started the wood stove, so don't let the fire go out." My father and mother proceeded to make the 30-minute commute into town to partake in some afternoon entertainment and discuss where they had gone so wrong as parents. (I made that last part up, but I wouldn't blame them for thinking it.)

My father only ran the woodstove when it got extremely cold, and the low was going to be single digits, which is uncommonly cold for Virginia. My brother, all alone for the afternoon, settled into the couch for a long session of Matlock reruns, when he was jolted into action by the sound of a bowl of dried flowers bursting into flames. He recounted later that it made a loud "whooooshhhhh" sound, and as he looked over - all he saw were flames. My mother had placed a cast-iron bowl full of dried flowers onto the wood stove for decoration. After a few hours of heat, these flowers would transition from beautiful decorations to a raging inferno of destruction. My brother looks over, and flames were reaching the ceiling within seconds. As he tells the story, it looks like the room is on fire. He instinctively grabs the cast iron bowl of flames and runs for the door. Luckily, he can get the fire out of the house and throws it into the yard where he then gets a hose and puts out the fire. My brother received minor burns on his hands and forearms from carrying the raging display of flames outside. He was so afraid of leaving the house for fear of additional penalties he chose to wait at home until my parents return. He did not want to add insult to injury - literally.

Upon my parent's return, they noticed a smoldering pile in the front yard. Upon entering the house, they found my brother with cold, wet wash clothes around his arms and a black stain on the ceiling of our stove room. My brother sheepishly explained the entire event. The Matlock, the whooshing sound, and his daring evacuation of the bowl of flames. He had saved the house from burning down. He had saved all of the family's worldly possessions, and he had effectively gotten my parents to completely forget about the "event" that had occurred a mere 16 hours earlier.

A few days later, as my mother was applying some ointment to his burns, my brother sensing an opportunity for a pardon, sweetly asked if he could go out with his friends this coming weekend. My mother said yes. (what is she going to say - she is applying ointment to the arms of the guy who saved all of her worldly possessions.) It appeared to me that keeping our home from destruction was a great tactic to erase a night of high school debauchery.

As the older brother, it was my job to get the sentence re-instated. I remember asking my father why he got out of his punishment. I reminded my father of the police at the house and the chaos that was caused by a string of poor choices, and that wouldn't it be better to make sure my brother learned his lesson. I was confused. It seemed that a foundational principle established in our home, you are accountable for your actions, was being tossed aside. It was an interesting conversation for my father and me to have because I had just turned 21, and this was one of the first truly "adult" conversations between the two of us.

It felt like I made a solid argument for the reinstatement of my brother's punishment. My father paused and then began to speak. He agreed with me about my brother's action and his need to be accountable, but he then said something that has never left my memory. He said, "Your brother saved this house from burning down, and he put himself in harm's way to do so. My intense disappointment has been replaced by extreme gratitude. I don't have space for both feelings, so I am choosing to stick with gratitude."

My father wasn't some all-forgiving, father of the year candidate. The chemistry of his brain was overpowering him. Human beings can't experience two opposite emotional states at once. Yes, a person can be grateful and happy, but a person can not be grateful and angry. It is impossible to be fearful and joyful at the same moment. A human can transition quickly between emotional states, but two opposite states can not exist at once. We all understand this principle from an early age - and it is this truth that even toddlers recognize in their parents. My son tries to get me to laugh when he is in trouble. His brain understood that if he could "get dad to laugh" that more than likely, the previous transgression would be wiped away by a healthy dose of humor.

A person's emotions exist in a binary state, and this truth can be used to prime your emotional state. Tony Robbins, a world-famous thought leader, and inspirational speaker utilizes gratitude to enable successful binary conditions. One of his processes is to begin his day by thinking of three things that he is grateful for. It could be a person, a thing, an experience, anything that makes him grateful. Now, he doesn't merely think of these, but he works to feel them. He recreates, to the best of his ability, those grateful moments and vividly re-experiences the things that fill him with gratitude. Gratitude is an amazing emotion because it creates a form of thankful happiness. It is not a selfish positive emotion like excitement, surprise, or joy. Gratitude gives you the same buzz of emotions like excitement, but these emotions stem from a place of thankfulness. The feeling makes you realize you are part of something bigger and reinforces that you are fortunate to have specific opportunities.

I have been trying this for a few months now, and I have been surprised how well it works to keep me in a positive place all day. Gratitude for me has more staying power than happiness, pleasure, or optimism. Gratitude has more firepower to fight off the negative emotions over a longer period of time. Gratitude is a simple emotion that creates stability throughout the day. I have experienced first-hand how gratitude can fend off negative emotions.

Tony Robbins isn't the only guru to subconsciously embed binary principles into key life strategies. Tim Ferris, best selling author, and world-famous experimenter, recently noted in his *Tribe of Mentors* book that, "Life punishes the vague wish and rewards the specific ask." Tim is imploring people to ask more specific questions. He challenges people to be specific with questions, specific about the people to whom you would pose those questions, and specific about the goals that come about as a result of those conversations. Tim has observed, tested, and confirmed that specific beats general.

Binary processes control our emotional state. The binary coding that controls our emotions made me question how our brains control the other functions. In my effort to dig into the power of binary, I was intrigued to discover that the entire human body is a complex organism dependent upon binary logic. Every genetic characteristic in the human body is an expansive series of genes that are expressed in a state of on or off. At the cellular level, our bodies depend upon millions of binary impulses that determine every aspect of our human experience. Even the wiring of the central nervous system responds to binary impulses. The neurons that control the messages at the microscopic level send one of two signals to our body - go or stop. Every thought, every decision, and every fiber of your neural network runs on binary signals.

Our internal circuitry utilizes the power of binary rules. Modern, 21st-century life is quietly shaped by endless rows of unseen "1" and "0" strung together over and over again. The invisible force of binary processes regularly enables the achievement of extraordinary outcomes through an unnoticed level of simplicity. The simplicity of binary processes conquers a world of complexity, one line of code at a time. If binary processes are responsible for the human genetic representation, neural level thoughts, and the entire technology revolution - what gives? Why is binary so great? What is it about binary processes that make it the central feature in complex systems?

Binary processes are simple, and we know that simple process doesn't take much effort, are fast, can be applied to situations broadly, and are repeatable. Binary principals promote the principle of practice. At a biological level, we see that our existence is dependent upon the firing of microscopic neurons over and over again. Repetition is a necessary function in the pursuit of excellence. Binary processes allow for consistent practice, and it is in the practice that enables mastery. It is through the repetition that binary processes create consistency. Consistency leads to automation. Binary systems allow for the automation of processes, and as the systems become more automatic, they function faster and with less effort, which allows for effortless access. We now know through enhanced brain-scanning technology that as neurons fire over and over together, they get faster and stronger just like a muscle. Muscle fibers are built up by being torn down and built back up. Neurons do not re-grow, but neurons do improve performance by repeatedly firing together over and over again. The neurons get into the habit of working together.

Nature, religion, and technology successfully produce beauty, wonder, and greatness due to a common set of principles (simple and binary). The foundational skills supporting any successful person is the ability to make binary decisions over and over again. Unlocking any potential requires an operating system that will allow for decisions to be simplified and then repeated until those decisions become automatic.

The simplicity of choice is critical to the repetitive nature needed to become excellent. The next section will provide the four decision rules that can form the foundations for anyone to achieve great results. These four rules can be consistently and successfully applied to any decision with guaranteed positive outcomes.

SECTION THREE

THE RULES:

The previous section set out to prove that the human brain is not wired to regularly make logical, forward-thinking decisions. The recent advancement in technology further exacerbates poor decision making. The same brain that is wired to keep you alive is also wired to change, grow, and adjust. Humans were made to adapt, to change, to improve. With the availability of the world's most powerful tool, your brain, the difficult reality is that you need to employ a new system. The example of such a system is all around us and found in the simple binary systems that create the foundation for almost every system we experience on a daily basis. Binary processes are fast and can be applied to a broad range of situations.

To better understand how simple processes would facilitate an easier decision-making process, consider the metaphorical image of a double-pan balance. This type of scale has two pans that are balanced against each other. The scale functions like a see-saw, with each of the two pans attached to a beam over a centered pivot point. Imagine this type of scale represents your life outcomes: family, job, health, spirituality. When the scale is in balance, your life outcomes are excellent. The catch is that to balance the scale; you only control the weight added to one of the two pans. The weight appropriated to the other side of the scale is controlled by life forces of which you have no control. These life forces might be things like race, gender, DNA, origin of birth, wealth, technology, and the actions of other people.

Some people struggle with a disproportional amount of weight stacked on the life force side. (race, gender, wealth, etc.) Regardless of the amount of weight being added, the reality is that everyone is working to balance their scale. Life forces are always working, adding weight, and creating imbalance, thus limiting positive outcomes. The side of the scale we control is brought into balance by one thing - our decisions. We can balance the scale through the choices we make every day. Each decision acts as a counterweight to the uncontrollable forces stacking weight across from us. Our decisions are the sole force that can bring balance to the unrelenting and unyielding distribution of weight being added by the life forces that oppose our success. Complex efforts to add weight to our metaphorical side of the scale are not practical. Our weight must be added quickly, and in order to accommodate the need for quickness, the decisions must be simple and flexible. We know that binary solutions are the answer. Our best weapon to balance our scale can be found in the building blocks of biology, religion, and technology.

Very rarely do we have the fortune to stumble upon decisions reduced to a binary state. Most decisions present themselves as complex, complicated, multi-leveled, non-linear choices. These large, unyielding decisions are impossible to place on our scale. The only chance to balance the scale requires us to reduce our decisions to the simplest form. By reducing the decisions to a simple binary form, we can quickly stack our side of the scale with the required amounts of weight to obtain the balance to achieve great outcomes. When decisions remain in the complicated, complex form, they tire out our System 2 brain and leave our System 1 to respond to what feels best. If we don't intentionally reduce decisions down to a simple form, we are misled by the biochemistry of our brains. The more complex the decision, the longer it takes our brains to wade through the unnecessary aspects of the options. The longer the decision takes, the less likely a good decision will be made.

The importance of reduction is most often seen in the mathematical world of fractions. Imagine you could win $50 million by completing one of the two math problems listed below. The math problem must be solved in under 10 seconds. The good news is that you have the power to pick which problem you will solve.

PROBLEM 1 - - $75/525 + 12/42 + 5,125/7,175 + 89/623 = X$

PROBLEM 2 - - $1/7 + 2/7 + 5/7 + 1/7 = X$

It is safe to assume that Problem 2 would be an overwhelming selection. In actuality, the problems yield the same answer, and the only difference is that Problem 2 has been reduced to a common denominator. The rules for adding these individual fractions are simple. The math to calculate the numerator (top number) is simple 2nd-grade math. To get Problem 1 correct, the person is must first determine the common denominator. Next, they will then have to reduce each numerator to the lowest form. The person will then be required to add those fractions together. In Problem 2, the person must perform a straightforward task. Problem 1 requires completing four complicated mathematical computations correctly and then combining those newly reduced numbers to arrive at the answer. Not only is this math in problem one proportionally more complicated, but also the time required to undertake problem 1 becomes an issue. The more straightforward math Problem 2 is faster to complete and easier to process.

People too often fail to reduce complex decisions to their most basic form. By leaving decisions in the natural state of complexity, a person must contend with complicated mental manipulations and evaluations. These evaluations are problematic for two reasons. First, we aren't good at them. The statistical principles are not easily accessible. Second, these evaluations tax the limited resources of our System 2 brain. The effort is wasted deciding, and so when energy is needed to act, the well is dry. These mental evaluations take time and create opportunities for personal, unforeseen bias to sway the final decision.

Simple, binary processes can be used as the basic building blocks of complex structures, as evident in biological cells, muscles, technology, and spirituality. Binary decisions rules work and can be used to reconstruct how humans make everyday decisions. As our world becomes more complex, we must balance the scale with simplification and that simplification is achieved through the binary decision rules that ultimately unlock the Hard Choice Habits.

The following section explains the specific rules which become the building blocks on which every outcome is built. These rules work to balance the scale and provide each person with a strategy to combat the human tendency to take the easy path. The rules are:

TO or FOR

BUT or AND

FEAR or FORWARD

These three Binary Rules represent the simplified state of nearly every possible decision. If a person could somehow "pre-set" their decisions on the choice of FOR, AND, and FORWARD their decisions would be significantly improved. These simple decisions would transform life outcomes from negative to positive, from bad to good, or from average to extraordinary. While all three of these rules are reduced to a basic form, there is one rule that serves as the foundational rule. EASY or HARD.

Hard Choice Habits build upon this rule. Every decision in life can be reduced down to EASY or HARD. This foundational rule for binary decision making will ultimately determine every life outcome. The other three rules build upon the reality that in every choice one option is HARDER than the other, and it is this HARDER option that leads to growth, advancement, improvement, and ultimately results in complete contentment

7

EASY OR HARD

"There are always two choices, two paths to take. One is easy. And its only reward is that it's easy."

Unknown

The 2015 book *Antifragile*, author Nasim Talib, hypothesizes that the most powerful systems and objects benefit from stress. He calls these objects and systems "antifragile." He contends objects and systems fit into one of three categories: fragile, resilient, or antifragile. Fragile items are damaged or destroyed by stress (example – china/teacup). Resilient objects are neither helped or harmed because of stress (example – plastic cup). Antifragile objects benefit from stress (example –

immune system). Objects and systems that are antifragile are improved from the presence of stress. It turns out that antifragile items need stress to meet their full capabilities. The stress builds, develops, fuels, and ignites features and benefits that would not be present without the availability of stress. Conversely, the absence of stress would limit the object.

"Wind will extinguish the candle, but will feed the fire." This quote serves as the perfect illustration of an antifragile object, the fire. The slightest wind can quickly snuff out a candle. Any sudden movement extinguishes the flame. But the same gust of wind that extinguishes a candle, fuels a fire.

The question then becomes, is the wind helpful or harmful? The answer has nothing to do with the wind. The critical question is understanding the perspective of the object. The first question must be, are you a candle or a fire? The designation, candle or fire, determines the evaluation of the wind. Many people make this common mistake and focus on the stressor and not the object under stress. We focus on stress because stress is not pleasant. Stress creates difficulty. Stress is HARD.

Human beings work tirelessly to avoid stress, and constant stress will eventually break even the strongest of us. However, in today's modern world, most people work to avoid all stress, even the most slightly acute stress. Humans prefer the easy path forward. Very few people will purposefully choose the harder option. Are we missing opportunities by always searching for the easiest path? Has our society done itself a disservice by promoting the allure of the easy path? Do we miss out on the growth by focusing on finding the easiest path forward? Taleb would say yes, the biological world would say yes, and the academic community would argue the answer is yes.

When I picture a truly HARD thing, I think about the process it takes to become a Navy Seal. The grueling process to become a Seal is legendary. Experts estimate that of the thousands of young men and women that enter BUD/S training, only 25% go on to become full members of the Seal unit. The hardest part of the process is "hell week." Hell week sorts the "haves" from the "have nots." The week is riddled with exhaustive physical challenges. A recruit's body is forced to respond in conditions that should make the body unusable. (cold, wet, sore, tired)

Hell Week is usually five and a half days during which candidates train for 20 hours a day. In these five and a half days, it is estimated that the candidates run over 200 miles and may sleep only 4 hours. Their bodies are pushed to near hypothermic levels, meant to break the spirit of anyone not mentally tough enough to continue. Yes, the physical challenges are daunting, but as many former Seals have described, to make it through hell week is all mental. Caloric restrictions are not a method used to challenge the spirit of the recruits. Upon further research, the lack of food would impact the recruit's physical performance, which is not the primary goal. At this stage, recruits hoping to be Seals are physical studs. The true test of Hell Week is to see which recruits have the mental resolve to keep moving forward, to not give up, to finish. The Navy wants to determine who will make the HARD choice over and over again in the face of extreme fatigue. At some point, walking will become a HARD choice. The soldiers are wet, chaffed, cold, and tired. The successful completion of the manufactured stress of Hell Week transforms strong soldiers into elite warriors. The mindset achieved from advancing through Hell Week gives the newly made Seal confidence and courage that could not have been achieved without the extreme conditions created by the stress. Soldiers who become Seals are antifragile, and it is this characteristic that will serve them in real-life battles to come. The Navy uses HARD choices to find men that are anti-fragile.

Many recruits lament that the most difficult part of the training was the lack of sleep and cold water work. The human body requires three core needs to be met to thrive - food/water, warmth, and sleep. The food and water are self-explanatory. The warmth is a requirement as a result of our status as mammals. We can not regulate our body temperature, so we must have clothing and shelter to protect us from the elements.

While food replenishes the body, sleep replenishes the mind.

The importance of sleep was proven during a study of implicit bias. Individuals were instructed to play a video game that tested a person's bias towards shooting minorities faster than they shoot non-minorities. Random participants were challenged to participate in this study, and it was found that minority perpetrators were shot more quickly than white perpetrators. The research proved the existence of implicit bias. The next natural progression of this experiment was to see how police officers performed this task. The new narrative about the predominance of bias within police departments would lead you to believe police officers would also show signs of implicit bias. However, police officers did not show signs of bias. Police officers scored in a way that shows their training and practice helps them to avoid implicit bias, with one major caveat. These officers performed flawlessly when they were well-rested, but if the officers were tired, they slipped back into the same range of implicit bias as the general population. The lack of sleep out weighted their training, and so these heroes were reduced to mortal status and made mistakes based on implicit bias. The lack of sleep affected their ability to perform.

By combining the lack of sleep and the drastic body temperature fluctuation, the Navy puts extreme pressure on the mental state of each recruit. The entire process is meant to do one thing, make the recruit quit. The drills are purposefully short. By being short, soldiers mentally have to choose to start and stop drills over and over. The process allows for a high number of opportunities for every soldier to "get off the ride." A recruit who will successfully evolve into a SEAL must hourly choose HARD over EASY. It is this mental automation of selecting the hard option that will form the foundation for the entire existence of a SEAL.

A person who repeatedly makes the HARD choice is considered to be a disciplined person. Successful people are described as having will-power, being gritty, or having resolve. These are people that have figured out a way to delay gratification and manage their System 1 brains. They are more emotionally intelligent and have much better situational awareness. They see the end goal and will not be easily stopped in their pursuit. There is a misconception that these types of people are gifted with special DNA. But in reality, these individuals aren't born, they are made. Willpower, discipline, grit, or whatever you want to call it is created through the practiced decision to choose the HARD option over the EASY one.

Discipline, willpower, and grit are excellent skills that can create foundational success in every aspect of life. It is for this reason that potential Seals are tested for the ability to make the hard choice. The impact of making the HARD choice is not just good for Navy Seals, but the overwhelmingly positive impact of selecting the HARD option is proven out by rodents and old school Ivy leaguers.

Psychologist Robert Eisenberger of the University of Houston hypothesized that when people do one set of hard things, they are more likely to do other hard things. Dr. Eisenberger put rats in one of two groups. He put some rats in a "hard" group. These rats were required to perform a hard task before they earned one pellet of food. The hard task was to press a heavy lever 20 times to get one pellet. The group of rats in the "easy" group only had to push the same lever twice to get the same amount of food. After several trials, Dr. Eisenberger observed that the rats from the "hard" group demonstrated more vigor and displayed more endurance in pursuit of the next task. He developed many variations of the same experiment, which was to make a group of rats work hard and give a different group of rats an easier path. His discovery proved that by having to work hard to be fed, the rats would train harder in other sessions. The rats in the hard group began to show the ability to working harder than the groups of easy rats. The rats rewarded for their hard work seemed to have the value of hard work imprinted into their neural wiring. It was as if they knew that hard work would lead to positive outcomes, so they simply keep pushing forward. They continued to make the hard choice.

The exponential impact of choosing the hard thing by pushing forward has been quantified in human beings as well. In 1940, Harvard researchers were interested in understanding the characteristics of healthy young men. These researchers were curious to see if they could develop a process to make young men happier and more successful. The researchers developed a treadmill test. The participants were asked to run on a treadmill set at a steep incline for up to 5 minutes. There is an aspect of physical health that is tested in this experiment, but the real test was to see how many participants would stay on for the entire 5 minutes. The test wasn't about cardiovascular endurance, but it was about the participant's willingness to push through the pain and not give up. The researchers were trying to determine the strength of will or the ability to continue to choose HARD over easy. A curious researcher named George Vaillant wanted to see whatever happened to the men who completed the treadmill test. By this time, the men who initially took the test were now in their 60s. Vaillant discovered there was a correlation between high run times and a large number of other success metrics. Men who had long run times seemed to have adjusted better psychologically through adulthood. These men made more money, took less sick days, used less mood-altering drugs, and self-reported more satisfying marriages. The treadmill test had indeed been a great determiner of adult success. The success had nothing to do with their ability to run 5 minutes on a treadmill, but the success was connected to the decision required to keep running during those 5 minutes.

The culmination of success over a long period of time is considered greatness. People who make it their jobs to study what it takes to be great have stumbled into an interesting debate about the world's peak performers. Malcolm Gladwell made the "10,000 hours rule" famous in his book Outliers. Mr. Gladwell argued that there is a minimum number of hours that are required to be "great." He argued that without crossing this threshold, greatness is difficult, if not impossible, to achieve. He sited examples like Bill Joy, Bill Gates, Steve Jobs, Mozart, and the Beatles. As a result of the success of this book, people gravitated to the number 10,000. Articles were written, blogs posted, and people everywhere started to do the math to see how many hours they had put in the bank to amass the required 10,000 hours.

While Gladwell highlighted quantity (10,000 hours), Anders Ericsson argued for quantity and quality. The godfather in the study of elite performance is K. Anders Ericsson, and it is Ericsson who originally formulated the 10,000-hour rule. Ericsson discovered the difference between really good and great is not just the number of hours, but the intentionality of the practice during those hours. While Ericsson believes greatness is found in practice, he also believes that it will take more than just hours of general practice. Ericsson has proven that the type of practice matters. Ericsson coined the phrase "deliberate practice." Deliberate practice consists of focused training on smaller aspects of the overall event. Deliberate practice is tiring and requires planning. Focusing on smaller aspects of the performance requires a level of detail that is not found in typical practice. Deliberate practice is not just going through the motions but is the accumulation of focused effort on small aspects of the event.

The common thread that connects both of these viewpoints is the underlying HARD choice. Whether it is the sheer volume of 10,000 hours of practice time or the focused effort of deliberate practice, both tactics require HARD choices over and over again. If you support the general "10,000 Hour Rule", you have to be very specific about your time. A formula to get 10,000 hours of practice could consist of 6 hours of training per day, six days a week, for five years. However, if six hours a day is just too much, because of work or of school, reducing practice time to 3 hours per day, which will extend the number of years needed to accumulate 10,000 from five years to ten years. The first HARD thing becomes the ability to get in the time required. A person will have to wake up early, turn down social opportunities, stay home from parties on weekends, practice after work into the evening, and make countless HARD choices just to make time for practice. The mere commitment of getting the 10,000 hours is an insanely HARD choice. A person must have mental and physical endurance to continue to make these choices over and over again for years to accumulate 10,000 hours. All the while, the pressure to accept the EASY path will be dangled before you daily.

If you follow Ericsson and agree that these hours of practice require another layer of effort called deliberate practice, the total number of HARD decisions required is far greater. Not only do you have to make the same amount of HARD decisions to make the time for practice, but deliberate practice is much harder than just your run of the mill practice. To engage in deliberate practice, a person must think about the drills to perform the deliberate practice. Then, the repetitive motion of the tiny aspect of the practice must be endured. Endured is the right terminology because deliberate practice is painful. By focusing on the small detail of an event, you are removing the fun from the event. It no longer looks like this fun, cool thing you enjoy. Now it is work. It is tedious. It is HARD. Deliberate practice transforms regular practice into a cascade of HARD decisions. For that reason, I am prone to support Ericsson's concept because his logic supports my model that the presence of HARD things is the key to success. Ericsson's theory increases the sheer number of HARD decisions, so the more HARD things you do, the more likely you are to impact the overall outcome.

Whether it is Navy Seals, rats, or Ivy league men, the benefits of making the HARD choice are clear. By choosing the hard choice, you are firing neurons that will allow for pathways to be built. These pathways will, over time, allow for the HARD decision to be made with more ease. People that make hard choices unknowingly put their brains through a form of practice usually described as "discipline," "will power," and "delayed gratification."

There is a common misconception that discipline is a trait. Either you have it or you don't, so as one pursues more disciplined habits, it becomes very frustrating to try and then fail. The failure stops many people from trying again. We must understand that discipline is built through the continued repetition of inherently HARD things. Discipline is real, and yes, some people are hard-wired to be more disciplined than others. Real behavior change requires the persistent presence of HARD decisions made over an extended amount of time. People become frustrated that they can't string together a series of HARD choices to create a sense of discipline, but the challenge lies in a person's ability to reduce the goal into single instances of binary choices - EASY or HARD. If you have pre-determined your choice, then when the decision point arises, you can focus on doing the HARD thing, not deciding what to do.

Society celebrates the achievements of great people. We all know these people, the ones in books, on the internet, and covered on podcasts. Unfortunately, the public only sees the accomplishment and not the thousands of hard choices that bring into existence the great achievement. Without viewing these choices, the public is uninformed of the trials associated with producing greatness. Everyone wants the short cut. But it takes the work, and its most simple format the work is choosing the HARD path over the EASY one. Without the regularity of HARD choices, advancement will elude even the most passionate person. People want outcomes without the painful callouses created by HARD choices. The HARD choice is painful, scary, and does not guarantee the hoped for desire. Achieving ultimate success in any endeavor is a manifestation of thousands of HARD decisions a person makes when no is looking. In every scenario, there is an easier option and a harder option. The HARD decision makes greatness possible. The EASY option offers temporary relief but is hollow of substance. While in the moment, every single HARD decision may not be directly connected to greatness, but the total sum of HARD decisions will greatly improve your outcomes over the long-run. Better relationships, better careers, more money, and greater satisfaction with life, are fueled by the catalyst of HARD choices.

8

BUT or AND

"Don't dwell on what went wrong. Instead, focus on what to do next."

Dennis Waitley

Psychoneuroimmunology is the study of the interaction between the human body's psychological processes, the nervous system, and the immune system. This relatively new field (abbreviated to PNI) takes a very interdisciplinary approach and incorporates 13 areas of study in an examination of the connection between the mind and the body. The critical point of intersection for those who study PNI is the interactions between the nervous and immune systems. This new

107

field works to quantify the relationship between mental processes and health outcomes. Scientists in this field are proving that your mental state and how you view yourself can impact your immune system. This field study's how your psychological stance affects your overall health.

King College conducted a study of 57 women with breast cancer in similar stages. The women were interviewed and placed in one of two groups. A person in this study would either be labeled a "fighter" or categorized as "hopeless." The "fighters" believed they would live long, full lives, even though they have a deadly disease. They believed they would beat cancer and come back stronger than ever. The "hopeless" women believed that they would soon come to the end of their lives. They thought they would leave behind their loved ones, and that they had had a death sentence. These "hopeless" women saw no reason to think there was a future or any chance of living. The results of this long-term study were staggering. Seventy percent of the women who were deemed "fighters" were alive ten years later, while only twenty percent of "hopeless" women were still alive.

This study highlights two key issues; first, your thoughts have the power to impact your physical condition. Second, the study underscores the impact of positive thinking. It made me wonder, in the framework of the Hard Choice Habits, what is the simplest decision one can make to remain positive. What is the pre-set rule to make sure a person is moving towards a more hopeful future versus becoming stuck in the limitations of their current reality? Thus, leading to the binary rule - BUT or AND.

We all know that person - the "yea, BUT" person. This person seems to find the downside to every situation. In real life, there are uncontrollable downsides to nearly every situation. People need to be aware of the pitfalls associated with relationships, ideas, activities, and plans; however, "yea, BUT" people are stuck in a limited mindset. The word, BUT, creates hurdles to the positive direction of everything. Think about the word, BUT in almost any situation:

- "She is pretty, but not as pretty as her sister."
- "It is a gorgeous day, but this humidity is just awful."
- "We could try that idea, but we have done something similar in the past that produced awful results."
- "I love my husband, but he is not good at the handyman stuff."
- "I would love to go to college, but I don't have enough money."

The decision of BUT promotes a limiting mentality for people that are too focused on the constraints defined by past experience. BUT is the passive-aggressive presence of fear, and is used to justify remaining in a safe place. BUT is used to derail change. BUT thinking, whether internal or verbalized to a group, serves as the governor that slows advancement. BUT is a snare that entangles progress and impedes progress.

BUT has such a strong shelf life because the statement that follows BUT is not inaccurate, and the descriptive facts surrounding BUT are factual. If my wife is not a good cook, that is the truth. It is not imaginary that college is out of the question due to a lack of funding. When your co-worker says, "BUT we tried something like that two years ago, and it didn't work," they are not making that up. BUT highlights a certain level of reality. BUT emphasizes the obstacle to a hoped-for place. BUT focuses the energy on the problem, not the solution.

For thousands of years, our brain has been wired to perceive danger and make sure we avoid being eaten by a sabretooth tiger. We have developed unconscious understandings of the world around us to ensure the longevity of our species. Isn't that what BUT is? BUT is the first rustling of grass on the edge of the savanna before the tiger pounces. BUT is the subtle change in the wind that predicts the storm will soon arrive. To the modern man, BUT is the first clue that something is not right. It is the first hint of distress. BUT is not as direct as "stop, no, or won't." BUT is the muffled whispered of trepidation.

If BUT alters momentum AND propels it forward. AND is opportunistic and additive. AND means that you are moving to a place of increase. In the hours before Hurricane Katrina hit the coast of Louisiana, Wal-Mart CEO, Lee Scott, tapped into the power of the AND decision rule for the leaders who found themselves in the path of the hurricane. Mr. Scott said, "A lot of you are going to have to make decisions above your level. Make the best decision that you can with the information that's available to you at the time, **<u>AND</u>**, above all, **do the right thing**." (Scott didn't know it, but he used the BUT or AND binary rule.) Scott knew the approaching storm would create unforeseen, complicated scenarios that could not be managed by the corporate office. He knew that these complicated scenarios would evolve quickly and that there would be no time for local leaders to "see what corporate says." The last seven words in Mr. Scott's instructions created a fast, simple, rule that could be applied to every situation . . . "and, above all, do the right thing."

Mr. Lee's binary rule and the dedication of these local staff teams set the stage for Wal-mart's stellar performance in the face of tragedy. The unintended binary decision rule created by the Wal-mart CEO empowered leaders to take bold steps in the goal of

111

helping the local community. Store managers allowed emergency personal to take supplies as needed, without paying for them. Many stores acted as headquarters for local police. One local General Manager broke into her own pharmacy to supply the local hospital with medicine. Another Wal-mart leader ran a bull-dozer through her own store to collect undamaged supplies so that she could give them away to members of the local community. The binary rule of AND ignited acts of bravery and guided the staff choices to do the right thing. As leaders were forced to make a decision, they simply used one filter in determining what to do.

Imagine that a relationship, idea, project, or situation is represented as FORCE. We know that FORCE = Mass (times) Acceleration. In this decision rule, introducing BUT into the formula, you are negatively impacting the acceleration. BUT adds a zero to the equation. You are slowing the force down, forcing it to change directions, or in many cases stopping it altogether. By decreasing the acceleration, you are lowering the energy. The resulting deceleration reduces the idea, relationship, or project to a level that cripples the outcome.

Carol Dweck, the famous author of *Mindset*, writes about the study she conducted to determine how praising effort, not talent, impacts performance. Her research was conducted by separating students into two groups. The first group, labeled the smart group, was given easy math problems to solve. Once they solved these problems, the students were congratulated for solving the problems because of how "smart" they were. The second group, labeled the "hard-working" group, was praised for working hard on the problems. The students were then given harder and harder problems to solve. The researchers discovered an interesting fact as the students worked on each problem. The hard-working students appeared to have an AND mentality. These students had a mindset that underscored a level of tenacity, which made them believe they could figure the problem out. They believed that it was not smarts that unlocked success, rather effort. The mindset seemed to be completely different in the students that were praised for being smart. These students seemed to have a "but" mentality. The students labeled as smart seemed to put self-created limits on their abilities. These praised for being smart, used this classification to come up with excuses. They approached the problem as if "smart" limited their opportunity.

Not only did the "hard-working" group keep trying, but the study also found that the participants in this group study self-selected more difficult puzzles and worked on the puzzles longer. At the simplest level, they kept moving forward. The "smart group" picked easier puzzles and gave up sooner. It seemed that when the children were told they were smart, that they fell back into BUT mentality. If you approach a problem from a stance of effort, you approach it with an AND mentality you push through. "This problem is hard, and I know that if I try one more time, I can get it."

At the most reduced level, these students were making AND or BUT decisions. The smart group believed they had limits. The believed "smart" is a predestined quality like tall, fast, strong, or female. Smart has a celling. In an attempt to slow down before hitting this ceiling, the "smart kids" used BUT to decelerate, saving their egos from a crash. "I could do the last problem, but not this one. I am not smart enough." Conversely, by believing that success is based on the controllable release of effort, the hard-working group had been empowered by AND thinking. As the world became more challenging, they looked for a new path AND knew they had the power to exert the necessary amount of effort towards their ultimate goal.

The epitome of AND thinking can be most easily observed in people who survive despite all of the odds stacked against them. These stories frequently occur when people battle Mother Nature. The backdrops of these stories are in the ocean, on a mountain, or in a remote forest. In 1996 a group codified the events of survival situations. The researchers found that in nearly every event, the disaster was made up of three parts. There was the condition. The condition is some form of outside event - a rogue wave, a sudden unexpected storm, or some sort of equipment failure. Then comes the act. The act is the pivotal moment when the path of normalcy is no longer available, and the characters are thrust into the path of life or death. The act could be the first "big mistake," or it could be the natural results of the condition. Finally, survival events are constructed of judgments. These are the decisions that people make at critical junctions that determine the final outcome. It is in these judgments that determine life or death.

Steve Callahan was hoping to cross the Atlantic alone. He designed his boat and paid great attention to each detail of his trip. Steve had made all the right decisions preparing for his trip. However, a condition occurred outside of his control. He believes a whale struck him, so only a few hundred miles into the trip, and his boat began to sink. The decisions he made over the next three weeks saved his life. He kept his lifeboat attached to his sinking boat as long as possible. This gave him time to think and reassess the situation, which allowed him to dive back in and gather necessary supplies. He decided to drink one ounce of water per day. He knew he would float 1800 miles, and he knew that he would need about three weeks of supplies. He made small plans and kept things intensely focused and simple. These small acts allowed him to focus his mind and give him a sense of accomplishment.

Steve believes the key to his survival was that he never wondered, "Why me?" He focused on what he could control and made sure to be fully present in his execution of those tasks, no matter how minuscule. "Why me?" is the internalization of BUT. Steve could have thought, but my boat sunk with all of my supplies, but 1800 miles is so far, but drinking one ounce of water per day will not sustain me. Steve chose to have an AND mentality.

There are countless stories of survivors that make AND decisions and are alive because of that mindset. Nick Williams became lost while hiking. He spent three days in blizzard conditions, no food, no water. To make matters worse, he stepped in a stream and froze his feet. He credits his son for saving his life. He decided he would survive AND see his son again. Juliane Koepcke fell 20,000 from an airplane and lived. If surviving the fall wasn't amazing enough, she landed in the dense mountainous jungles of Peru. She knew that rescuers would never see her, so she decided to follow a river AND save herself.

Researchers have found that 75% of people who die in a survival situation die in the first 48 hours. Many of these victims have enough supplies to live much longer than 48 hours. Another intriguing clue to making it out of a survival situation is found in the fact that children under the age of 6 have the highest rates of survival. All of the research proves that survival is not based on someone's experience, mental aptitude, or the gear they have. Survival is based upon decisions made in response to ever-changing conditions. It is believed that children under 6 are such good survivors because they have limited understanding of the likelihood of a truly horrific outcome, thus staying focused on just listening to their bodies. If they are tired, they sit down. If they are cold, they huddle under some leaves. Unfortunately, once a person has the mental capacity to be fearful and can imagine the possible negative scenarios that are possible from their current situation, they begin to spin. They overthink, react to emotion, or become indecisive. Survival comes down to remaining in control of even the slightest task to keep oneself alive. It is about forward momentum, even if it is ever so slight. Nick Williams remembers thinking, "**And** all I have to do is make it to the morning, **and** then the sun will be up, **and** then I will be warm, **and** then I can be rescued. This self-talk is filled with AND thinking. Nick forced himself to focus on the freeing mobility of AND. This cultivation of his self-talk saved his life.

Epictetus wrote, "On occasion of every accident that befalls you, remember to turn to yourself and inquire what power you have for turning it to use." AND creates the necessary power to consider a new perspective. AND inspires hope. It plants a seed that, when fertilized by the right perspective, can grow into an unshakeable oak tree.

9

TO or FOR

"The things which hurt, instruct."

Benjamin Franklin

Researchers at the University of California did a study in which they placed a single cell amoeba into an environment with perfect conditions. The petri dish had the right temperature, the proper lighting, the right humidity, and the availability of the ideal amount of food. This little amoeba had the inside track to a struggle-free, great life. The usual challenges that hinder the growth of one-celled amoebas were no longer an issue, so it was nothing but smooth. Sadly, the story does not end so well for our one-celled friend. Even though the conditions were perfect, the amoeba died.

More recently, Daniela Kaufer, an associate professor at UC Berkeley, challenged our perceptions about stress. In her study, she found that some types of stress are a good thing. She discovered that specific amounts of stress push you to the perfect level of alertness and allow you to improve your behavioral and cognitive performance. The study explored how acute stress (not chronic stress) could impact performance. Researchers found when rats were subjected to stress their performance did not immediately improve, but performance did improve two weeks after the stressful event. The researchers contended that the extended time is needed for the neurons to mature and officially wire together. The brain seems to learn from the stress, and then the neurons wire together as a result of the stress, ultimately leading to improved performance on a long-term basis. Dr. Kaufer concluded, "Stress can be something that makes you better, but it is a question of how much, how long, and how you interpret or perceive it."

Even one-celled organisms need challenges to grow. A person's ability to withstand stress is dependent upon the intensity and duration of the stress. Each person also approaches stress differently based on genetics and environmental factors. These items are outside of our control. You can't control the intensity and duration of stress, and you can't control your genetic make-up. But you can control how you interpret stress.

At the most basic level, you must decide if something is happening TO you or is something happening FOR you. These are the pre-set binary rules that will help you to interpret the unavoidable stressors we all experience. This rule is all about perspective. As difficult things occur in your life, you can look for the growth opportunity in each episode, or you can wallow in the difficulty of the situation. By deciding that things happen FOR you, you have now re-positioned your perspective to look for the positive opportunities that could result from any negative stress.

Norman Garmezy was a developmental psychologist at the University of Minnesota. He is credited with being the first to academic to study the concept of resilience. Norman would visit schools and ask to meet children who came from troubled homes. He would ask to meet with the children that have all of the red flags for being problem students, but were adaptive and successfully making it through school. He would seek out the kids that were overcoming the stress of their home life and succeeding despite those challenges. The research Dr. Garmezy started was advanced in 1989 by psychologist Emmy Werner. Dr. Werner published the results of a 32-year longitudinal study, and after three decades of observations, she found that several elements predicted whether or not someone would be resilient.

The study found that resilient people responded to stress in a certain way. Resilient children "meet the world on their terms." These children had a strong belief that they could affect their achievements. They believed they had the power to set their own course and make adjustments along the way, regardless of the obstacle in front of them. Dr. Werner's discovered that resilience could change over time. She found that resilience ebbed and flowed and wasn't a constant calculation. It was a unique, personalized, time-stamped equation that compared the perceived stress levels to the level of resilience at that moment. We all have a breaking point, but that breaking point is not a fixed point. Werner's findings prove that resilience can be developed, strengthened, and then strategically used to advance successful personal outcomes.

The key to the development, strengthening, and deployment of resilience is your perspective on the event. When researchers compared how kids who are lost in the wilderness faired, they found that inner-city kids did better than suburban kids. Inner-city kids are used to dealing with predators and tougher situations, while the suburban kids are experiencing predators for the first time. Said differently, when left in the wilderness to fend for themselves, the inner-city kids have a level of resilience that has been developed based on their surroundings that the suburban kids don't have. By circumstance or choice, resilience is not a gift, but a trait that can become developed.

In his book, *David and Goliath*, Malcolm Gladwell states that "there is unexpected freedom that comes from having nothing to lose." Anytime we think of a "David" character, we think about the scrappy little guy who had all the reasons to fail but refused to lose and slain the giant. Gladwell's book was all about resilience. Gladwell discusses the idea that there might be such things as "desirable difficulties." This phrase, while counter-intuitive, was coined by Robert and Elizabeth Bjork. A desirable difficulty is a task that requires a considerable but desirable amount of effort. The required effort is first seen as a hindrance, but the long-term benefits of persevering through the hindrance far outweigh the benefits of avoiding the difficulty altogether. Gladwell uses dyslexia to illustrate a type of desirable difficulty.

People with dyslexia use more of the right side of their brains, which is the conceptual side. You don't need conceptual support to read. You need precision to read strings of words. Dyslexia also creates problems in the way people hear. People with dyslexia struggle to pick up the slight differences in letter sounds. The conceptual side of the brain is not adept at doing specific work to notice details that distinguish sounds from one another. People who struggle with Dyslexia are at a considerable disadvantage in learning how to read.

Somehow, thousands of people who have dyslexia succeed despite their challenges. People that struggle with dyslexia are forced to develop unique strategies to navigate our cultural education system. A system that is unintentionally positioned to cause their failure. This learning disorder requires a mix of creativity, resourcefulness, stealth, and risk-taking to continue to progress through the system. Individuals with dyslexia struggle from the time they enter school. They continually practice non-traditional skills that allow them to navigate a world they are not genetically prepared to navigate. This practice becomes a habit, and these habits allow them to overcome academic difficulties. The same habits that help them barely get through traditional school settings enable their success in the business world. It is the inverse of why gifted children often fail to live up to their potential. Gifted kids have the smarts, but they often lack the academic challenges that created resilience in children with dyslexia. So at the first sign of trouble, which may not arrive until they are in their late teens or early 20's, these gifted children are unable to push through difficult situations. They start to believe that difficulties have happened TO them. They become stuck and never use their God-given talent to achieve any significant level of accomplishment.

I knew a guy in high school who was brilliant. He never made below an A, was in all of the gifted classes, but never really studied. He breezed through grade school and was accepted to four good colleges. He went to college and finished the first semester with a .02 grade point average. I joked with him that I didn't even know that a GPA could get that low, but he assured me it could. He decided to come home and enter the workforce. He bounced around from job to job for a few years. Finally, he decided it was time to do something with his life, so he enrolled in the Navy. He scored off the charts on his ASVAB. The recruiter told him he could pick any field he wanted. He chose Nuclear Engineering. If he served for six years, he could come out of the service with a Nuclear Engineering degree and start a civilian job making $100,000 minimum. It was a great opportunity. In the weeks leading up to basic training, I asked him if he wanted to work out to get ready for boot camp. He said he didn't need to worry about it that he was doing some stuff and didn't think it was a big deal. By the third day of boot camp, my friend had quit. The physical requirements were too demanding. My friend flunked out of the service.

As I reflected on his situation, it is apparent to me that he was never required to struggle. He was never required to build up his mental, spiritual, or physical toughness. Things came to easy to him, and when life turned up the heat, he left the kitchen. I imagine no one would want their child to have dyslexia, but I wonder in a quiet moment if you asked my friend's parents what they would have answered. Dyslexia would have forced him to struggle, to strive, to fail, to preserve. This "nothing to lose" situation would have given him the FOR perspective he needed to handle real-life difficulties.

Using difficulties to propel yourself forward is such a fantastic perspective to have. I have always been impressed to hear people who go through devastating situations, but once through the worst of it, these people would not change the past. These people illustrate the power of a FOR mentality. Dr. Beck Weathers was a part of an expedition to scale Everest. In 1996 he was part of the now-famous group who ascended to the summit and then got caught in a treacherous blizzard. Twelve people died, and Beck's life would be changed forever. Because of the severe frostbite, Dr. Weathers lost the fingers of his left hand, his right arm up to his elbow, and lost his nose. He should have died on that mountain, but didn't. An interviewer once asked if he would like to have his hands back? Beck replied that he would like to have the use of his hands again, but if he had to go back to who he was before the accident, he would not want his hands. It sounds like Beck realized that his accident happened FOR him. It changed him and made him a better father, husband, and person. Life is much more difficult to navigate without hands, but Beck has the perspective to understand that through his ordeal, he gained so much more. He could never have gotten to that position if he had remained stuck in a TO mentality. To see the good from this unbelievably difficult situation, he had to adjust his perspective to believe that this accident happened FOR him.

Desirable difficulties force your perspective to shift. You no longer have a choice, you have to approach the solution from another angle, or you may die. The good news is that we don't have to go through a life or death experience to achieve a FOR mentality. By starting with a FOR mentality, a person can create a perspective that sees even the toughest situations as an opportunity. If a person purposefully takes every bad situation, every failure, every unfair experience, and sees through the difficulty of the growth, then true greatness can be reached. By actively choosing to apply this rule in small, controlled situations in everyday life, one avoids the possibility of learning this rule through one harsh lesson.

I travel on an airplane quite a bit for my job, so I have had my fair share of airline delays and cancellations. The worst of these delays is when travelers are forced to stay overnight and take a flight out the next day. The logistics of these overnight delays create considerable amounts of frustrations for everyone involved.

During one of these overnight delays, I was once in the line to get my hotel voucher, and everybody was grumbling. It was 11:00 pm, everyone was tired and pissed. As I was complaining with the woman in front of me about the perils of air travel, I noticed the gentleman behind me was smiling and seemed as happy as can be. His positive attitude pissed me off more.

Didn't he know that outrage was the requirement? How dare he "have a good attitude." I asked Mr. Smiles A Lot why he was so happy. His answer staggered me. He preceded to tell me that he views these situations (flight delays, sitting in traffic, or being made late due to his wife's tardiness) as God keeping him from a worse fate. He shared that when he found out that night that the flight was delayed until the next day, he said a prayer of thanks. I was baffled. I asked him why he would be thankful. He explained that he believed that the delay happened FOR him. He said that he imagined that the delay was God's way of keeping him safe. He looked around and then said in a very hushed tone, "I remain positive because I think that if not for the delay, the plane would have crashed, and we would all have died." He believed everything happened FOR him, not TO him. He ended our discussion by reminding me that it was our choice that determined our perspective – FOR or TO.

Actions are the manifestation of your beliefs, and when you believe you are a victim, you act like a victim.

Actions will ultimately change your circumstances, but to gain the necessary progress, you must start with your perspective. Perspective allows humans to change how they view of any situation, but the next rule allows people to change their position. The FOR or TO rule is about a mental perspective. The next rule is about action. By understanding that something happened FOR you position yourself to reap the benefit of a powerful perspective. But to take advantage of this perspective, you must choose to move FORWARD.

10

FEAR or FORWARD

"You gain strength, courage, and confidence by every experience in which you really stop to look fear in the face. You are able to say to yourself, 'I lived through this horror. I can take the next thing that comes along."

Eleanor Roosevelt

There is nothing that strikes fear into a person like becoming a parent. In a quiet space, the reality hits me that the endless hours I have spent working on this book are a result of fear. I am afraid my children will make bad choices. I fear they will choose a darker, less prosperous path that is far more painful and challenging than the road I would choose. I fear that my failure as a parent will cause them permanent harm. This fear has driven me to devise a decision-making system that can be easily used. Fear is a necessary aspect of human existence. It has kept us alive and allowed our species to flourish for thousands of years. Fear buys us time, and it creates space between ourselves and danger. By giving "danger" more attention and making it more of a priority, we give ourselves a better chance to live.

Our entire bodies respond to fear. When we experience fear, our breathing and heart rates increase. Fear impacts our blood flow. Peripheral blood vessels constrict, while blood vessels around our vital organs dilate to flood these organs with oxygen-rich blood. Muscles flood with blood, so they are ready to respond to any threat. Our physical reaction to fear is something all of us have experienced, and even at an unconscious level, our bodies are aware of fear. Studies have shown that if you are shown "scary" sets of eyes, masked by visual noise for less than 2/100 of a second, your heart rate goes up. Your System 1 is very good at unconsciously sensing fear.

FEAR that our children could make even the smallest misstep, or experience the most trivial of displeasure has also transformed parenting in the 21st century. Researchers first noticed this change around 2013 and saw drastic changes with the iGen (not Millennials). The iGen is the first generation to be raised with a phone in their hand. Upon further examination, researchers found that these children had far less "free play" than generations past. The constant influx of information about germs, kidnapping, and tragic crimes created a system that stressed safety at all costs. While these safety systems have saved lives, their unintended consequences have created a generation of children who are over-parented and living in a state of "safetyism" that promotes safety over all other things. Experts argue that the iGen generation has not been properly exposed to risk. This risk-free existence creates young adults that are ill-prepared for disagreement and conflict. Learning institutions are creating "safe spaces" and requiring professors to identify "trigger words" so that students can prepare to be uncomfortable. Keep in mind that we aren't talking about work camps, prisons, or places where physical harm will be administered. We are talking about college classrooms. Some members of society feel the same level of angst when their beliefs are challenged as they would if they were in real physical danger.

If we are willing to accept the fact that our avoidance of stress results from fear, then we are required to address the issue of FEAR. We must decide to move FORWARD into the fear if we are to achieve great outcomes. Humans become focused on the specific aspects of the stress, pain, or dilemma we are facing; however, the area that needs our attention is in the acknowledgment of FEAR. We must first choose to do what frightens us. We must decide to move FORWARD into the obstacles between the place where we stand and the place where we want to be. The thing that kills great achievement is not the perils of the path, but the avoidance of the journey.

There is a story of a man who died and was being shown around heaven by St. Peter. As the two walked, St. Peter asked if the man would like to meet anyone. The man thought for a moment and then asked St. Peter if he could meet the greatest military general of all time. St. Peter agreed, and off they went to meet this great military mind. St. Peter and this man sat upon the bench as a figure approached. St. Peter pointed to the man in the distance who was the greatest general to walk the earth. The man was perplexed; he knew this man in the distance that St. Peter pointed out. The man exclaimed to St. Peter, "This is no great general, this man was my neighbor. He was the town baker, and he wasn't even the best baker in town." Saint Peter leaned toward the man on the bench and softly said, "You asked to see the greatest general of all time, and this is who I have shown you. Fear kept this man from his true destiny. His chains were the fear of failure, fear of change, fear of the challenge. He became comfortable in his kitchen, and chose to remain stagnant and lacked the faith to follow his heart and become all that God intended him to be." As the baker who should have been warrior walked by, the newest member of heaven sat thinking back on his life. He wondered if his fears had kept him from his destiny. He dared not ask and continued upon his tour.

Fear is unavoidable and inescapable. Even animals experience fear. A group of researchers conducted a study where four monkeys were placed into a room with a tall pole. Food sat at the top of the pole. As a monkey would ascend the pole and get close to securing the food, he would receive a blast of cold water. The soaked monkey would descend the pole and wait for the next monkey to attempt to climb the pole. The next hungry monkey would give it a shot. The second monkey would experience the same fate, and as he closed in on the food, he would get blasted with water. This process would happen to all four monkeys until none of the monkeys had a desire to climb the pole. In the next phase of the experiment, the researchers replaced one of the original monkeys with a new monkey. This new monkey was free from fear of water, would see the prize at the top of the pole, and take his shot. Ironically, the other three monkeys knowing the outcome would aggressively work to keep the new monkey from climbing the pole. The three original, fear-riddled monkeys would not allow the new brave monkey to climb the pole. Their fear broke the spirit of the new monkey, and after a few attempts, the new monkey was assimilated into the fearful norm. The researchers systematically replaced monkey after monkey until there were no original monkeys left who experienced the punishing spray of water. The new monkeys were living under an unseen fear passed on from their immediate social circle. These new monkeys wouldn't climb the pole, and didn't have the faintest clue why.

From this study, the worst part of fear is the ability for fear to be passed from one creature to another. We are afraid of things we have not even personally experienced. Not only do we allow our fear to impact our progress, but we must also contend with the fear of others pulling us backward. The intent of those who argue for safety is not ill-intended. The result of fear-based living is a life of stagnation. Nothing great was ever accomplished standing still. There is value in safety, but safety itself should not be the only factor in our judgment.

We become stronger because of the stress to tolerate and move through a fearful situation. But what about our psyche? How does stress impact our perception of the lives we live? Psychologist Dan McAdams studied two groups of people. One group had a higher level of pleasant life experiences. They were content through a large portion of their lives. Another group identified that their lives had quite a few negative stages, but then these negative stages reversed course and ended positively. These people who experienced negative periods in their life reported more satisfaction. The study found that people who endured a more stressful life were more satisfied than those who enjoyed a less stressful life.

The upside of enduring adverse outcomes should propel us FORWARD into fearful situations. The research shows that we should look for the experiences that cause us small amounts of fear and offer the potential for failure. We should make sure we feel slightly fearful. We should consider ourselves anti-fragile and look for opportunities to be stressed to grow stronger, but we don't. We don't change careers because we are afraid our family will judge our decision. We don't write the book, for fear of being rejected. We don't ask out the pretty girl, for fear of being told no. We don't stop the cool kid who is bullying the unpopular kid, because we are afraid of what our friends will think. We don't avoid fear because we are bad people. We are wired to avoid fear, which is why we must push FORWARD despite the fear.

The importance of FORWARD is most clearly observed in the biomechanics of our bodies. Your entire body is optimized for forward movement. Your joints, muscles, sockets, and tendons are all engineered to be most effective in forward motion. Imagine two runners racing. One is running forward, and the other is forced to run backward. The backward runner would not stand a chance. Think about two different scenarios involving jumping scenarios. The current record for the standing long jump is 12 feet 2 inches and some change; I would dare bet someone would be able to do a third of that backward. Now imagine running backward and then jumping. This task would require extreme athleticism, and most of us could not even run backward and jump 18 inches. The world record for the typical, forward-facing long-jump is 29 feet. The human body is designed to move forward. The simplest of physical movements humans perform, such as crawling, walking, and running, are more easily done in a FORWARD motion.

FORWARD not only gets us to where we want to go, but it also keeps us strong, sharp, and in tune with our environment. The action required in FORWARD creates strength, toughness, and resilience. This is true whether it is an actual FORWARD movement, or if it is moving FORWARD into a new area of business. It might be moving FORWARD into a new relationship. It might be moving FORWARD into a new phase of an existing relationship, like forgiving someone who has wronged you. It might be FORWARD into a new career. All of these decisions to move FORWARD will require your overcoming FEAR. Any FORWARD advancement involves the management of fear. We often highlight the fear of the unknown. The fear that might befall us if we move FORWARD, but fear is so cunning that fear attacks our caveman brain from both sides.

Fear will not only conjure up possible pitfalls unseen around the next corner, but fear will also remind you that you l stand to lose what you have right now. Now you have two things to fear - the fear of what might be and the fear of losing what you have. For fear to win, it doesn't have to stop you from moving FORWARD. It can be quite useful by just keeping you stationary. A stationary location feels safe. It is alluring to get to a comfortable stage in life and want to remain stationary. It is a reality that as you accumulate money, status, or anything you value that you will not want to lose it. We are made to look forward, move forward, live FORWARD.

Andy Grove was the famous CEO of Intel. Grove is credited with Intel's growth from revenues of $2,672 in 1968 to $70 billion in 2018. Grove is most famously associated with leading Intel from a manufacturer of memory chips into an industry-leading producer of microprocessors. Grove was born in Hungary to a middle-class Jewish family in 1936. The first two decades of Grove's life proved to be very difficult. Grove lived through Hungarian political upheaval, German occupation, the Nazis' "Final Solution," and a wide range of Communist regimes following the second world war. In 1957, Grove left Hungary and traveled to America. He knew very little

English, but earned his bachelor's degree in chemical engineering in 1960 and then got his Ph.D. in chemical engineering in 1963.

Intel's crucial decision was to move away from memory chips and move into the microprocessors. In 1985 Japanese memory chip companies were producing chips much cheaper, and this new threat was putting many of the US chip producers out of business. Intel had been considering a major strategic shift. The company had a huge choice to make. They could stay in the memory chip business or lay-off 7,000 employees to get into the microprocessor business. Andy Grove and Gordon Moore were sitting in Intel's Silicon Valley offices, contemplating this impossible decision. The co-founders, key leadership staff, and the board of directors had been debating the two options for weeks. As Grove sat with Moore looking out of the window, Grove asks Moore the critical question that would illuminate Intel's path forward. Grove asked Moore, "What would happen if somebody took us over, got rid of us - what would the new guy do?" Moore responded, "Get out of the memory business." Grove's question to view the choice through the lens of a new guy gave Grove the clarity to make the difficult decision. The complexity of the strategy was irrelevant, and the final decision of what to do was simplified to a binary option, FEAR or FORWARD.

There are countless examples of individuals that achieve greatness despite their fears. They accomplished great achievement because they committed themselves to move forward. These world-changing people acknowledge the reality of negative outcomes manifested in fear but decide to push forward. These great men in history did experience fear, but they choose to move FORWARD. Below are some of my favorite examples illustrating the power of FORWARD.

- Abraham Lincoln is known as the President, who preserved the Union. However, Mr. Lincoln had a staggering number of failures. He was defeated seven times for public office. He experienced the death of a girlfriend and a child. He failed in several businesses. He had a nervous breakdown, and it is believed he battled depression.

- Winston Churchill, considered a great British leader, held the line against the Germans and inspired a nation never to give up. Churchill was a poor student and almost didn't make it into college. As Britain's Secretary of Navy, he decided to attack Turkey on the Dardanelles coast. This attack was an utter failure, and he was dismissed from his position. Churchill was widely viewed as a failure by the age of 40.

139

- Thomas Edison is the world-famous inventor with 1,094 patents to his name. He famously claimed to fail 10,000 times in his attempt to create the light bulb, but his commitment to FORWARD was not built in his lab. Edison was labeled "too stupid to learn anything" by his teachers. He lost his first two jobs for not being productive enough.
- S. Truett Cathy, the founder of Chick-fil-A, created a company worth $4.5 billion. Mr. Cathy had to battle significant adversity on his journey towards success. His brothers were killed in a plane crash three years after they opened their first restaurant together. Cathy's second restaurant burnt to the ground, and Truett did not have enough insurance to rebuild. Soon after that, he was diagnosed with polyps on his colon and was out of work for months.

We love to talk about a person with a "conviction." Conviction in its purest state is the perpetual drive FORWARD. Conviction is best achieved by conquering FEAR, fear of failure, fear of losing status, fear of change. FORWARD is the willingness to step over fear, focusing on a future state of existence and then taking actions to assume the location of your future state. Our society is awed by big, impressive accomplishments. While these are inspiring, I am more intrigued by the small, daily FORWARD decisions that go unseen. Abraham Lincoln issued the Emancipation Proclamation to move our country FORWARD. However, it is possible that the most difficult thing he did on September 22, 1862, was to step over his depression and get out of bed. Publicly we understand the size and scope of his proclamation, but the small step of getting out of bed might have been more critical than the speech. FORWARD, like the other decision rules, is not a one-time, big-ticket decision that can cure all your problems. If a person cannot make small choices of FORWARD over FEAR they will never make it to the crossroad of the significant decisions that produce greatness.

SECTION FOUR

FROM THEORY, TO ACTION

Simple binary decision rules forge the foundations of The Hard Choice Habits. In the tiny moments throughout the day, a person can base their actions on the expansive attributes of the four rules. It is impossible to foresee every decision that will arise throughout the day. Our only certainty is that one choice will be more difficult than the other one. This book has set out to prove that regardless of choice, the best option is the HARD one.

To move this theory into action, a person must accept the reality that small steps can influence outcomes. We will make thousands of decisions each day, and there is no way that you can <u>always</u> choose the harder path. However, awareness of the opportunity to purposefully decide to make more HARDER decisions will improve your outcomes exponentially. The small choices of selecting the HARD path over the EASY path become critical in developing The Hard Choice Habits.

The power of small is evident when we observe how changing a single word can influence our outcomes. A professor at Harvard Business school gave her students a short amount of time to prepare a brief speech to give to their class. As you can imagine, many of the students were visibly nervous. The professor came up with two different priming statements. One group of students was told to repeat to themselves, "I am excited" before giving their speech. The other group was told to recite the phrase, "I am calm." The small difference proved to have quite an impact on a student's performance. The students who were "excited" gave speeches that were 17% more persuasive and appeared 15% more confident than the groups that verbalized "calm." People who told themselves "I am calm" before speaking in public throttle back the natural energy that is generated by speaking in public. In the process of throttling back this energy, the overall audience experience is negatively impacted.

Researchers found that when people face a simple temptation, the words they use to refuse the temptation can predict their likelihood to avoid that temptation. Researchers placed participants into two groups, the "I can't do that" group and the "I don't do that" group. The study found that the "can't" group gave into the temptation 61% of the time, while the "don't" group only gave in 36% of the time. This small change in self-talk impacted short-term temptation but also influenced long-term goals as well. Scientists studied people who wanted to regularly work-out and put them into two groups. As motivation began to dip, each group was asked to say different things. One group was told to repeat, "I can't miss my workout," while another group was told to say, "I don't miss my workout." The results were staggering. Eighty percent of the "don't miss" group stuck to their routine, while only 10% of the "can't" group stuck to their routine.

Dave Brailsford used the power of small to turn the British Cycling team into champions. Coach Brailsford developed his tactics from a strategy he called "the aggregation of marginal gains." Brailsford based this principle on the concept that if you broke down every aspect of riding a bike, and improved as many things as possible by 1%, that you could cumulatively access significant gains. Some of the small changes he used were: redesigning bike seats, wearing heated shorts to keep muscle temperature consistent, rubbing alcohol on tires for better grip, and testing a wide range of fabrics to find the most wind-resistant ones. The team was obsessed with examining every aspect of performance and making slight improvements.

The small changes worked, and in 10 years (2007 - 2017), British cyclists won the Tour de France 5 times and won 178 world championships.

Dan Chambliss is a sociologist who studied what separates great swimmers from average ones. He spent six years of his life studying swimmers at every level. He concluded that it isn't talent or God-given gifts that make great swimmers. He found the great swimmers were obsessed with the minute details of their performance. It wasn't as if great swimmers said, "I want to do a good turn." The great swimmers deconstructed every aspect of the turn and then practiced each of those aspects. Dan's research supports Erickson's belief about deliberate practice. Chambliss found that by focusing on small changes, a swimmer could make tremendous improvements. Dan said it best, "Superlative performance is really a confluence of dozens of small skills or activities, each one learned or stumbled upon, which have been carefully drilled into a habit." The Hard Choice Habits are the same principle without the waterlogged skin and chlorine riddled hair. The binary decision rules of EASY or HARD, TO or FOR, BUT or AND, FEAR or FORWARD become the dozens of small actions that become habits.

If you have ever begun a fitness regimen or trained for a physical challenge, you have experienced the power of small activities. Your new fitness goal highlights the unexpected effect of small efforts. We don't show up to the gym able to lift 400 pounds or run a 6-minute mile. In the pursuit of our fitness goals, we are required to start small with lighter weights and slower paces. The key to making our bodies stronger depends upon the small, repetitive exercises. Any physical improvement starts with the repetition of a weight lifting exercise or the continuous process of putting one foot in front of another. We take small steps each day to stress our systems, so they become stronger.

The decision rules are the small repetitive exercises that create the strength and stamina to build the decision muscle needed to achieve the biggest of goals.

11

THE DECISIONS MUSCLE

"Everything about our animalistic brains tries to compress the space between impression and perception. Think, perceive, act – with milliseconds between them. We can question that impulse. We can disagree with it. We can override the switch, examine the threat before we act. But this takes strength. It's a muscle that must be developed."

Ryan Holiday

Edward Taub is a behavioral neuroscientist working for the University of Alabama. The American Stroke Association has hailed Taub as a professional "at the forefront of a revolution." Taub has developed techniques to rehabilitate people who have suffered paralysis due to strokes or other neurological injuries. His method is called Constraint-Induced Movement Therapy - CI Therapy for short. Taub believes that after a person suffers a stroke, they experience "learned non-use" because using the affected limb is very difficult. CI Therapy forces the affected limb into use, thus allowing new neural pathways to form. These pathways become stronger with more focused effort, and as the neural pathways become stronger, the affected limb becomes stronger and more easily used.

Conventional stroke rehab typically occurs three days a week for about an hour a day. CI Therapy is made up of high repetitions of simple movements. Taub's treatment requires 6 hours of work per day for 10 out of 14 days. This type of therapy relies on a behavioral technique called "shaping." Shaping takes an incremental approach to accomplishing complex tasks. The adult patients undergoing CI Therapy look to be playing children's games by pushing large pegs into pegboards, grasping large balls, or picking pennies out of a pile and placing them in a piggy bank. These small movements are performed time and time again until the patient is exhausted. The goal of these games is to help patients re-learn how to move affected limbs. These small steps in therapy replicate the same small steps humans go through as babies and toddlers. These repetitive small movements rewire the brain so that the patient can overcome the "learned non-use" developed as a result of the stroke.

People throughout this world are experiencing "learned non-use" of their decision muscle. Because we believe that the volume of decisions we face each day is too great and too unpredictable. This victim mentality (that we are all guilty of) compels us to become a sort of decision couch potato. We decide on autopilot led by our reptilian brain just looking for what feels good. Life has been made easy through advances in modern technology. Our newly discovered "easy living" is not a bad thing. There are advantages to not having to grow our food and worry about getting eaten by bears. However, the easy life is not free. Mankind pays for this easy life with hundreds of millions of easy choices, and these easy choices ultimately lead to soft, flabby outcomes. Humanity has the technology to automate nearly every aspect of our life, but we cannot automate our decisions. Free will, without the shaping of hard choices, results in learned non-use of our decision muscle.

In 2018, David Goggins wrote the book "Can't Hurt Me." In this memoir, he told the story of how he was a lost, out-of-shape, twenty-year-old kid who turned himself into a hard-core Navy Seal, world-class distance runner, and successful author. (I highly recommend reading this book to learn more about his amazing story.) David credits his success to his "calloused mind."

> David writes, "The first step on the journey toward a calloused mind is stepping outside of your comfort zone on a regular basis. Dig out your journal again and write down all of the things you don't like to do or that make you uncomfortable. Especially those things you know are good for you. Now go do one of them and do it again. This is not about changing your life instantly, it's about moving the needle bit by bit and making those changes sustainable. That means digging down to the micro-level and doing something that sucks every day. Even if it's as simple as making your bed, doing the dishes, ironing your clothes or getting up before dawn and running two miles each day."

A calloused mind means having the mental toughness to make the HARD choice. Mr. Goggin tells that in order for him to become a Navy Seal, he first had to learn to swim. HARD. Then he had to pass a critical written exam to qualify for BUDS school. HARD. Due to injury, it took him three attempts to complete BUDS. (This means three hell weeks. Less than 20% of candidates make it through one hell week, let alone attempt three. REALLY HARD.) David believes that the callouses required to make it through 3 Hell Weeks were formed through the HARD choices of his past. David contends that the numerous, small hard decisions he had laid a foundation of toughness that allowed him to persevere through considerably harder situations (like Hell Week). David's hard choices of the past enabled him to power through his present hard choice.

A calloused mind is acquired through the daily exercise of your decision muscle, and the required exercises can be found in the form of the binary decision rules. The calloused mind is created by doing the HARD thing over the EASY thing. Callouses are formed when you bring an AND mentality to a situation. The work out regiment is built upon choosing the perspective that life happens FOR you, not TO you. The decision muscle works when you move FORWARD, despite your FEAR.

The binary decision rules create a regiment of purposeful practice. By focusing your energy on acting as opposed to deciding to act, you are now able to use these daily decision points as workout sessions for your decision muscle. The intentionality of reducing your decisions into binary scenarios creates small, manageable episodes that unlock an ability to practice making decisions. Like lifting weights to strengthen a muscle, these small decisions ultimately improve a person's ability to make decisions.

There is proof that other complex, non-linear systems are strengthened through stress – like a muscle. We have examples that show improvement is possible through the presence of stressors and that not only do the stressors help the complex system, but they are required to fortify the system.

Biological Immunity: The immune system was designed to learn and improve to protect human life from the ever-changing environment of our existence. The germs and viruses of today are much different than 200,000 years ago, so the immune system must have the ability to change and improve. The change is accomplished via exposure. The immune system must encounter doses of potentially deadly viruses and bacteria to reap the benefits of expanded vitality. It is the exposure that strengthens the immune system. The system can only become stronger after being exposed to new, potentially fatal strains

Parenting: An interesting thing happened in 2013. For the first time, more college students demanded books, speakers, and ideas be banned from college campuses than adults. Until this point, parents of college students had been the primary driving force behind on-campus censorship. Researchers discovered that this dynamic changed because of new parenting styles. The new parenting styles sometimes referred to as Helicopter

Parenting or Overprotective Parenting started with good intent. Parents began working hard to protect their children not just from obvious dangers (being hit by a car) but also protecting their children from perceived discomfort. As our society advanced, parents have made life easier for their children and intentionally or unintentionally limited young people (ages 3 - 18) to any possible discomfort – physical or emotional. Parents have worked to remove any stress from their child's life. This quote underscores how parenting should work: "Prepare the child for the road, do not prepare the road for the child." Many parents have prepared the road, and so once the child is on a section of the road not prepared, they are unable to thrive. Children need exposure to discomfort. Children need to experience stressful situations. Children need space to practice doing the HARD thing.

Courage: A Canadian psychiatrist, J.T. MacCurdy, examined the mystery of courage by studying how Londoners responded to The Blitz of 1940. The Blitz was the German bombing raid that lasted over an eight-month period. During this attack, German planes dropped thousands of bombs onto the city of London. Before these attacks, the British government was afraid that such an attack would not only kill hundreds of thousands of people, but politicians contended that the psychological damage done to the survivors would be far worse than physical death. Leaders worried that everyone would flee the city and that the economy would come to a complete halt. With the economy halted, English society as they knew it would fail to exist. The politicians worried that the people of London would be emotionally broken, and this brokenness would result in an unrecoverable state of panic.

Surprisingly, even after the death of 46,000 people and the destruction of close to one million buildings, the panic never came. This unexpected reaction of the Londoners was attributed to the stoic mindset of the British people. British people were proud to claim that their "Britishness" had allowed them to keep a "stiff upper lip" during the bombings. These amazing survivors believed their genetic code, influenced by geography, had strengthened their resolve to courageously with-stand the Blitz. Dr. MacCurdy would go on to prove otherwise.

In his research, he found the German attacks created three groups of people. People killed by bombs made up the first group. The next group was considered those who experienced "near misses." Londoners who fell into this group felt the percussion of the bomb, saw the devastation of buildings destroyed, and most likely were injured. These are people who feel they have just experienced a near-death experience and are thankful to be alive. The final group of survivors is the remote misses. People in this group see the bombers, hear the sirens, and can see the explosions in the distance. The remote miss people are not in any real danger and feel like they are in the "front row" of the action. Malcolm Glidewell summed it up best in his best selling book David and Goliath, "A near miss leaves you traumatized. A remote miss makes you think you are invincible."

MacCurdy discovered in his research that these remote misses created a form of courage that could not have been established without the stress created by the bombing. MacCurdy stated, "We are also prone to be afraid of being afraid, and the conquering of fear produces exhilaration . . . When we have been afraid that we may panic in an air-raid, and, when it has happened, we have exhibited to others nothing but a calm exterior. We are now safe, the contrast between the previous apprehension and the present relief and feeling of security promotes self-confidence that is the very father and mother of courage."

The Londoners of the 1940s were a tough bunch, but they did not survive the bombings because of their genetic heritage of having a "stiff upper lip." Londoners were not genetically predisposed to be more courageous than people from other parts of Europe. The Londoners did not have some magical treasure trove of courage before the bombing started. The Blitz created the stiff upper lip, and some historians have argued that the Blitz did more damage than good for

Germany's long term goals. The Blitz served as an unintentional catalyst that emboldens the British people. The bombs meant to destroy the city of London galvanized the spirt, and provided the fuel to stoke the fires of courage.

Adults often dismiss the power of practice and credit outside factors in both their accomplishments and setbacks. Londoners practiced courage every night. They showed up, calmed their children, reassured their neighbors, and lived their lives. These small decisions built their courage. The days of the bombings were undoubtedly hard, and so as the Londoners learned, the price tag for any new level of achievement is HARD choices. Every outcome requires a specific sum of hard choices. For the British to beat back the Germans, the entire country was required to make hard decisions every day.

Amy Purdy understands the relationship between achievement and the required sum of hard choices. Amy has put in quite a few "reps" in the pursuit of strengthening her decision muscle. Amy didn't have a choice and was forced to accumulate hard choices as a result of her unique situation. For Amy, the choice was either the hard path or exist in a life of despair and sadness. One day when Amy was 19, she left work with what she believed to be the flu. Twenty-four hours later, Amy was hooked up to life support and given a

2% chance of living. Amy lay in a coma, stricken with bacterial meningitis. Amy lost her spleen, her kidneys, the hearing in her left ear, and both legs below the knee.

Before her accident, Amy had a passion for travel and loved snowboarding, but her new body had her questioning her future. How would she travel the world? How would she get back on her snowboard to feel the cold air as she raced down the mountain? For months after leaving the hospital, she stayed in a depressed state of understandable sadness. Finally, she made the hard decision to figure out a way forward. Amy says, "Our obstacles can only do two things: one, stop us in our tracks, or two, force us to get creative." Amy knew she had to choose the hard path forward.

She had to design prosthetic legs that would allow her to snowboard again. She went back to work, and she went back to school. She created a foundation. She traveled the world, and she won two gold medals in snowboarding. Amy concluded a 2011 Ted Talk with the following challenge, "Instead of looking at our challenges and our limitations as something negative or bad; we can begin to look at them as blessings, magnificent gifts that can be used to ignite our imaginations and help us go further than we ever knew we could go."

Amy's current fulfillment, success, and perspective are not the result of some sort of special gift. Her attitude today is not related to her wealth or status.

Amy's outcomes in her personal and professional life were bought and paid for through the accumulation of hard choices. Amy has gone on the record to state that if she could somehow choose between the life she knows now or a life with her legs, she would choose her current life. Amy is now in a place to understand that her circumstances forced a cascade of hard decisions upon her, and it was her acceptance of the hard path that ultimately led to her incredible success.

I am ashamed to admit that when I hear stories like Amy's or David's, I experience a range of emotions. I am in awe of their accomplishments. I respect their mindset. I admire their resilience. I am impressed with their ability to repeatedly choose the hard option. But while I am inspired by their ability to come through the pain to a place of success, I am also oddly jealous of their opportunity. Their unique experiences, made possible by difficult circumstances, forced hard choices upon them. It was the accumulation of the hard choices that ultimately lead to success. The hard choices were required to make it through their trauma to a new place. Amy, David, and people like them achieve their current level of success because of their traumatic situation, not despite of them.

I wonder to myself in a state of doubt, would I choose that path? Would I want a road filled with difficult choices created by traumatic experiences? Is it wrong for me to consider people like Amy and David lucky? Did the hard decisions thrust upon them provide them a benefit that I have not been given? A sort of "hard choice privilege" that seems almost unfair. Is it fair that I have two parents and both of my legs? Does the inner-city kid, living in poverty, with no parents have the advantage of desperation? Is there a sense of freedom knowing that their situations, albeit amazingly difficult, leaving them with very few choices? Amy and David realized a certain level of freedom that comes with having nothing to lose, so the hard path became the only path.

I grew up with two great parents, a safety net of loving extended family members, good schooling, the epitome of a middle-class lifestyle. Because of this stereotypical "American Dream" life, did I miss the truly hard choices that would provide the opportunity to strengthen my decision muscles? Did the prosperity afforded to me as a result of the hard choices made by my forefathers limit my own outcomes? Did the hard choices of the generations before me eliminate the state of desperation?? And, if the answer is yes, would I roll the dice to test my spirit and pursue a hard path?

Humans live in a world in which many circumstances are out of their control. We cannot pick our family, where we are born, or our genetic make-up. People grow where they are planted. I had the fortune of being planted in a fenced-in garden, with good soil, prepared through the toils of my ancestors. Amy was planted in a similar garden but experienced a significant storm that altered the conditions of her environment, forcing her to make significant adjustments. David Goggins was planted in a rocky, tough area forcing him to develop a level of toughness that my fenced-in garden didn't require. All of us are required to adjust accordingly to our surroundings. Amy and David could easily point to singular moments that created their hard choices. However, most people (like me) may have to be more deliberate in the pursuit to strengthen their decision muscles.

A great irony of life is that the more successful we become, the easier it becomes to avoid hard things. Wealth, status, and position create an availability of easy options. The truth is that in most cases, wealth, status, and position require a high volume of hard choices. People will talk about "losing their edge." When a person "losses their edge," they have removed the friction required to sharpen their blade. They are making less hard choices as a result of their wealth, status, position, and are taking the easy options. The hard choices created the wealth, status, position, but now, in the absence of hard choices made on a regular basis, the blade is dull and can not cut through the dense undergrowth of life that keeps us from unlocking our full potential.

We exist in a world of mediocrity because a majority of the human race stops short in making the required number of hard decisions to pay for greatness. The absence of tragedy is a gift and a curse. This duality requires heightened awareness for those of us who have the privilege to go through life without regularly facing severe adversity. Those who live in a world of adversity are forced to deal with the hard choices, but those of us who do not must be more purposefully mindful to structure intentional hard choices into our everyday life. There must be an awareness of how we can strengthen our decision muscle by making hard choices.

12

STRENGTHENING THE DECISION MUSCLE

"I'm thankful for my struggle because without it I wouldn't have stumbled across my strength."

Alex Elle

These examples support my thesis that progress, advancement, and growth are correlated to the total sum of HARD decisions a person is willing to make. The examples are not exclusive, meaning that there are thousands of other studies and scientific examples highlighting the value in HARD things. HARD choices are undeniably impactful. The question becomes, how can the average everyday person purposefully engineer

HARD choices into their daily routine? Is it possible to plan HARD choices?

If we revisit the metaphor that your decisions resemble a physical muscle, the task of developing a plan becomes more realistic. Just as a plan is required to strengthen your muscular system, intentionality is needed to strengthen your decision muscles. Muscles are not made stronger without a work-out regimen that forcibly places the muscle under organized stress. The process of building up your physical muscles takes weeks, months, or even years. It is not done by accident. It takes a plan and the right exercises to apply the right stress to the right muscle to achieve the desired results. Decision muscles are no different.

EXERCISE 1 – HARD CHOICE THINKING

We know that we will have hundreds of opportunities each day to choose a harder path, but maybe action is too difficult. The first step in a focused work-out regime for your decision muscles might be a change in your thought pattern.

A recent study proves the power of thought. To understand the power of thought, scientists created an experiment using finger strength. Participants of the study were prescribed specific activities to see how these activities impacted the strength of the fingers. Subjects were broken into three groups. The first group

163

did nothing. The second group was given specific finger exercises to do. The final group was assigned the same list of exercises but was told to merely think about doing them. This third group didn't do a single exercise but rather thought about the exercises. The third group didn't just daydream about the exercises. The participants in the third group were instructed to spend the same amount of time thinking about the exercises as the group doing the exercises. The third group was told to visualize the exercise, see them, feel them – do everything short of doing them. The outcome was interesting. Obviously, the 1st group, who did nothing, did not see any gains in finger strength. Just as you would expect, the group that physically performed exercises did see an almost 38% increase in finger strength. Finally, the third group who just thought about exercising saw an increase of 21% in finger strength. It turns out that mental focus can impact the physical world.

Begin strengthening your decision muscles by purposefully thinking about a specific binary decision rule. I recommend focusing on HARD decisions because HARD is the foundation for all other rules. At the start of each day, we know a handful of the exact HARD decisions we will face. What to eat? How we will treat our family? How we will handle traffic? How we might have to have a tough conversation? How do we unwind at the end of the day? Or how we prepare for the next day? See these decisions in your mind's eye, and instead of thinking about the actual decision focus on doing the HARD thing

This type of decision-making rehearsal can take place anywhere. You can do this while you are getting ready for work, or while you are heading into the office. The key is to make sure that you are focused on the visualization of the decision and create the mental image of the decision. To the best of your ability, you must feel yourself in that spot, having to choose path A or path B. You must think about the emotions you will feel at that key moment of decision. Think about the logical reasons to choose the easy path and then remind yourself of why the harder path is required. Argue with yourself and play devil's advocate.

EXERCISE 2 – DOING HARD THINGS YOU ENJOY

You can practice doing HARD things throughout the day in areas you enjoy. I often use this strategy while working out. I like working out. I enjoy pushing myself. However, sometimes towards the end of my workout, I have a desire to slow down, to not work as hard. When I feel myself pulling back, I remind myself that I do HARD things. I say this to myself a few times and push through until my workout is complete. I try to do the same thing with food. If I am at lunch and considering the extra-large helping of french fries, I will often look at the salad and think – I do HARD things. I then order the salad. I find that when I purposefully practice the seemingly mundane HARD things, I am more prepared to make the HARD choice when confronted with a truly important decision. By making HARD decisions in areas I enjoy, I am better equipped to make the HARD choice in areas that are inherently more difficult. I use my daily enjoyable, less important HARD choices to prepare for the unpleasant, meaningful HARD choices.

EXERCISE 3 – MEDITATE

Meditation is the purposeful act of emptying your mind. This is hard. Your mind is in a constant form of chatter so that as threats present themselves, you can avoid those threats and remain alive. Meditation quiets the mind and controls the inner dialogue of the primitive brain. It is the required control of the inner dialogue that supports making the HARD decision. Meditation, at its simplest form, is binary. You either empty your mind to nothingness, or you allow the signals of the outside world to implant thoughts into your mind's eye. Your entire being works to take external signals and pass them along to your conscious mind to make you aware of possible threats. It is HARD to fight off every biological cell in your body to benefit from the state of meditation.

It is no surprise to me that the most successful people I know meditate. The power of meditation is impactful because meditating creates two benefits with one act. First, meditating restores your mind and acts to cleanse the clutter that is accumulated by your never quiet monkey brain. The second, often overlooked benefit, is that meditation forces your brain to do something HARD. The mental state of quiet requires disciplined focus, which is hard. The spiritual benefit of quieting your mind is well documented, but the ability to meditate correlates directly to the ability to make better decisions. By controlling the physical impulse of thought, you are unintentionally strengthening your decision muscle. The entire time you are meditating, you must decide not to think. Blocking out the thought is one continuous exercise of your decision muscles. Every action is a result of a decision, so mediation is the purest form of exercise a person can do to increase the focus of the mind.

EXERCISE 4 – SPEAK TO THE PRESENCE OF HARD CHOICES

My wife and I have developed a family mission statement. One of the tenets in our family mission is, "In this family, we do hard things." We try to bring this to life in a wide range of ways. We try to ask our kids each day to tell us one hard thing they did today.

As you can imagine, the answers we get to these questions cover a wide range. We get the humorous, hard choices, "It was hard to eat my vegetables tonight." And we get the heart wrenching hard choices, "Nobody ever sits with Suzy at the lunch table, so I sat with her today." We discuss hard choices not taken, "I didn't do well on my test, and so I should have studied more instead of playing on my iPad." We also attempt to underscore the presence of hard choices in critical aspects of daily life. We point out that the value of trying new things is that new things are accompanied by hard choices. We remind our kids that change is good not merely for change's sake, but because change presents us with an assortment of hard decisions. We try to remind our kids that practice – whether it is soccer or multiplication – is an opportunity to work through hard things.

The growth isn't in the change, the trial, or the opportunity. The growth is in the presence of the difficulty that accompanies the change, whether that change is perceived as good or bad. Verbalizing this reality grounds you during good times and inspires you during the bad. Verbalization of hard things highlights the value of hard choices and reinforces the resolve to accept the lesson taught in hard things. It creates intentionality that multiplies the impact of every situation. The goal is to increase the number of hard choices made daily. The more a person talks about, acknowledges, identifies these hard choices, the more likely they are to choose the hard path. Being comfortable with HARD choices will make HARD decisions less scary and more easily attempted.

EXERCISE 5 – SEVEN ADDITIONAL HARD CHOICES EACH DAY

Thinking is good, but change occurs through action. Improvement is possible through the catalyst of decision. Franklin Roosevelt said, "There are many ways of going forward, but only one way of standing still." Life's most significant opportunity requires action, and the quality and combination of these actions will determine the outcome.

Seven HARDER decisions per day generate 49 HARDER decisions per week, which over the course of a year makes 2,548 HARDER decisions. By focusing on the small repetitions, a person can train their decision muscle to be stronger and have the necessary power needed when life becomes difficult. The idea of making seven hard decisions a day quantifies the theory and creates a process for people to strive to meet a goal. By mindfully focusing on when, how, and what type of HARD decisions you make, you are actively engaging your brain in the growth of your decision muscles. Over time, the effort required to make HARD decisions will be lessened, allowing a person to increase the number of

HARD decisions from 7 to 14 or allowing them to
handle intensely more HARD decisions.

Break your day up into sections, and consciously
use the binary rules to drive key decisions. Even though
we never know the exact moment a decision is required,
we do have some general ideas as to when specific
opportunities to make hard decisions will materialize.

6:00 am . . . HARD Decision 1 - Wake up 20 minutes
early to meditate.
7:00 am . . . HARD Decision 2 - Eat Oatmeal and Fruit,
not a bagel.
10:00 am . . . HARD Decision 3 – In the staff meeting,
add to any discussion by using the word "and."
12:00 pm . . . HARD Decision 4 - Order salad for lunch.
3:00 pm . . . HARD Decision 5 - Send your significant
other a nice text - just because.
6:00 pm . . . HARD Decision 6 - Cut off the tv, put your
phone down and play a board game with your child.
9:00 pm . . . HARD Decision 7 - Sit down and reflect on
your success or failure related to making seven better
decisions and plan out tomorrow's seven decisions.

The goal starts with 7 HARDER decisions per
day, but continued growth will require that number to
grow over time. The number 7 is the starting point.
Greatness is directly correlated with the sum of hard
choices, so as you continue to strengthen your decision

muscle, you will need to increase the volume of purposefully hard choices. The analogy of physical training continues to apply. When you are training to run a marathon, you don't just run 2 or 3 miles. Marathon training requires that you continue to add miles to your training in a purposeful manner over the weeks preceding your event. Training your decision muscle will be the same. At some point, seven will need to be increased to continue to achieve the desired results.

CONCLUSION

The Hard Choice Habits are built upon the application of binary rules that reinforce the value of struggle and can simplify our decision to embrace the struggle. These same types of simple rules power the forces of nature, technology, and religion. The impact of binary processes offers a level of hope as we look to make better decisions. By accepting the presence and power of binary decision rules, we are given a chance to interceded against millions of years of evolution and create habits that unlock our fullest potential. By simplifying our options, we can use these rules to create a habit which allows us to improve the outcomes in every phase of our life.

These principles can act as the foundational elements of a dependable, functional decision-making process.

We make poor decisions because we fail to practice and are mentally drained by the constant stress of the outside world. Our decision muscles are not prepared for the stress and strain of hard decisions at critical inflection points along the unique journeys of life.

Whether in your personal or business decisions, the one guarantee is that at times mistakes will be made. Failure will occur. This process of decision making allows for continual practice, but progress will come in the form of two steps forward and one step back. Don't get discouraged when you take that step back. Continue to work your decision muscle by accessing the binary decision rules. The power of these simple rules is anchored in their ability to be used hundreds of times per day. By consciously developing hard choice habits in what appears to be mundane, inconsequential decisions, we are strengthening the required elements of our decision-making network to perform when the consequential decisions arise.

I hope that this work has inspired you to view HARD choices as opportunities and that you will purposefully structure your day to benefit from the multitude of HARD choices you will inevitably experience. The presence of unlimited opportunities of daily practice can be a tremendous advantage as we progress towards fulfilling our life's unique purpose. These HARD choices only become an advantage when we leverage their value to propel us forward. It is only with the acceptance and conquering of HARD things that a person can unlock their fullest potential. Picking the easy path lulls us into an unfulfilled state of existence. Easy choices make us less then we can be, ultimately diluting our cosmic impact.

Every person was made to be great at something, but it is only through HARD choices that you can unlock the greatness that God has sown into your being. You have the seed, the water, the sun, but your metaphorical field requires toils. The toils required to reap the ultimate harvest are your sweat, your tears, your soreness, your discomfort, all which collectively are HARD CHOICES. The toils can be paid daily or can be avoided daily. Each day that you avoid these toils, you only make the next days' work that much more difficult.

While I don't pretend to know the specific greatness God has planted in you, I do know that for this unique seed to bear fruit, you will have to commit to the toils of HARD choices. So why wait? Why put off the HARD choices? If not for you, then what about for your children, your friends, or even strangers. The world is depending on your HARD choices to usher in a gift that only you can produce. Accept this reality, do the HARD thing, bear the fruit only you can bear, and make this world a better place.

Book Notes

Chapter 1

- Jacopo Prisco. "Why UPS trucks (almost) never turn left." cnn.com. Cable News Network. February 23, 2017. Web.
- Mike Brewster. *Driving Change: The UPS Approach to Business*. New York City: Hyperion, June 12, 2007. Print.
- Leonard Mlodinow. *Subliminal: How Your Unconscious Mind Rules Your Behavior.* New York City: Vintage Books, 2012. Print.
- Brian Wansink and Junyong Kim, "Bad Popcorn in Big Buckets; Portion Size Can Influence Intake as Much as Taste." *Journal of Nutrition Education and Behavior 37,* no 5 (September and October 2005). Print
- Adrian C. North, "In-Store Music Affects Product Choice," Nature 390 (November 13, 1997) Print.
- George Markowsky. Encyclopedia Britannica. "Physiology". britannica.com/science/information-theory/physiology. Encyclopedia Britannica. Web.
- Nick Saban and Brian Curtis. *How Good Do You Want to Be?: A Champion's Tips on How to Lead and Succeed at Work and in Life.* New York City. Ballantine Books, January 23, 2007. Print

- Malcolm Gladwell. (2017, June 29). Miss Buchanan's Period of Adjustment. http://revisionisthistory.com/episodes/13-miss-buchanans-period-of-adjustment. Podcast.
- Jason Grissom and Christopher Redding. "Discretion and Disproportionality: Explaining the Underrepresentation of High-Achieving Students of Color in Gifted Programs". January 18, 2016 https://journals.sagepub.com/doi/full/10.1177/2332858415622175. Web.

Chapter 2

- Harper Lee, *To Kill a Mockingbird.* New York City: Harper Lee, 1960. Print.
- Plato, *Phaedrus.* Indianapolis: Hackett Publishing Company, 1995. Print.
- Daniel Kahneman, *Thinking, Fast and Slow.* New York City: Farrar, Straus, and Giroux, 2011. Print.
- Richard Thaler, *Misbehaving – The Making of Behavioral Economics.* New York City: WW Norton and Company, 2015. Print.
- Richard Thaler and Cass Sunstein, *Nudge.* New York City: Penguin Books, 2008. Print.
- Jonathan Haidt, *The Happiness Hypothesis.* New York City: Basic Books, 2006. Print.
- Chip Health and Dan Heath, *Switch.* New York City: Broadway Books, 2010. Print.

- Roy F. Baumeister, Ellen Bratslavsky, Mark Muraven, and Dianne M. Tice. "Ego Depletion: Is the Active Self a Limited Resource?" Journal of Personality and Social Psychology. (vol 74 – No. 5) pages 1252 – 1265. Print.
- Jeremy Berg, John Tymoczko, and Lubert Stryer. *Biochemistry, 5th Edition.* New York City: WH Freeman, 2002. Print.
- Shai Danziger, Jonathan Levav, and Liora Avnaim-Presso. "Extraneous Factors in judicial decisions" Proceedings of the National Academy of Sciences of the Unitve States of America. https://www.pnas.org/content/108/17/6889.short. April 26, 2011. Web.
- University of Newcastle upon Tyne. "'Big Brother's Eyes Encourage Honesty, Study Shows." ScienceDaily. ScienceDaily, 28 June 2006. www.sciencedaily.com/releases/2006/06/060628091247.htm
- Paul Whalen, "Human Amygdala Responsivity to Masked Fearful Eyes White," Science 306 (2004): Print.
- Thomas Gilovich, Robert Vallone, and Amos Tversky. "The Hot Hand in Basketball: On the Misperception of Random Sequences." Cognitive Psychology 17, 295-314 (1985). Print.
- Chapman University. "America's Top Fears 2016." Wilkinson College of Arts, Humanities, and Social

Sciences. October 11, 2016.
https://blogs.chapman.edu/wilkinson/2016/10/11/ame
ricas-top-fears-2016/. Web.

- Paul Meehl. *Clinical Versus Statistical Prediction.*
New York City: University of Minnesota, 1954.
Print.

- Fritz Strack, "Inhibiting and facilitating conditions of
the human smile: a nonobtrusive test of the facial
feedback hypothesis.", Journal of Personality and
Social Psychology. May 1988 volume 54. Print.

- John Bargh, Mark Chen, and Lara Burrows,
"Automaticity of Social Behavior: Direct Effects of
Trait Construct and Stereotype Activation of Action."
Journal of Personality and Social Psychology 1996.
Vol 71, No 2. Print.

Chapter 3

- Harsha Reddy. "https://bluelist.co/blog/google-stats-
and-facts/." Bluelist.com. Bluelist. June 13, 2019.
Web

- Pew Research Center.
"https://www.pewresearch.org/internet/fact-
sheet/mobile/." Pew Research Center. June 12, 2019.

- Martin Hilbert. "The World's Technological
Capacity to Store, Communicate, and Compute
Information." Science. April 2011 Vol. 332. Print.

- Ian Chaffee. https://news.usc.edu/134580/internet-use-at-home-soars-to-more-than-17-hours-per-week/. USC News. January 22,2018. Web.
- Simon Sinek. https://www.youtube.com/watch?v=sL8AsaEJDdo. Inside Quest. December 12, 2016. Web
- Michael Grandner, Rebecca Gallagher, Nalaka Gooneratne. "The Use of Technology at Night: Impact on Sleep and Health." Journal of Clinical Sleep Medicine. February 2018. Volume 9, Issue 12. Print.
- Alyson Gausby. http://dl.motamem.org/microsoft-attention-spans-research-report.pdf. Microsoft. Spring 2015. Web
- Walter Mischel. "The Marshmallow Test." New York City: Little, Brown and Company, 2014. Print.
- Charlene Li and Josh Bernoff. "Groundswell." Boston: Harvard Business Press, 2008. Print.
- Bill Tancer. "Click." New York: Hyperion. 2008. Print.

Chapter 4

- Covenant and mitzvot. https://www.bbc.co.uk/bitesize/guides/zfwr97h/revision/3. BBC. January 1, 2019.
- The Fox and the Cat. https://fablesofaesop.com/the-fox-and-the-cat.html. Fables of Aesop. March 25, 2019.

- Andrew King and David Sumpter. "Murmurations." Current Biology 22 No. 4. 2012. Print.
- Herbert Simon. "Administrative Behavior: A study of Decision-Making Processes in Administrative Organizations". New York. Macmillian. 1947. Print.
- S.P. Luby et al. "Effect of Handwashing on Child Health: A Randomised Controlled Trial." Lancet 366. 2005. Print
- Norbert Schwarz et al. "Base Rates, Representativeness, and the Logic of Conversation: The Contextual Relevance of Irrelevant Information". Social Cognition 9 (1991). Print.
- Gerardo Okhuysen and Kathleen Eisenhardt. "Integrating Knowledge in Groups: How Formal Intervention Enable Flexibility." Organization Science 13. No. 4. 2002. Print.
- Daniel Kahneman, *Thinking, Fast and Slow.* New York City: Farrar, Straus, and Giroux, 2011. Print.
- Donald Sull and Kathleen Eisenhardt. Simple Rules. Boston: Houghton Mifflin Harcourt, 2015. Print.
- Atul Gawande. The Checklist Manifeston. New York: Picador. 2009. Print.

Chapter 5

- Anders Ericsson and Robert Pool. *Peak: Secrets from the New Science of Expertise.* Boston: Houghton Mufflin Harcourt, 2016. Print.

- Fearless Soul. https://www.youtube.com/watch?v=v-DcCsbGt0g. May 16, 2017.
- Tim Ferris. *Tool of Titans.* New York: Houghton Mifflin Harcourt, 2017. Print
- Norman Doidge, M.D.. *The Brain that Changes Itself.* London: Penguin Group, 2007. Print.

Section II
- The Tim Ferriss Show. "Jim Collins". Number 361. February 18, 2019. Podcast.

Chapter 6
- Brandon Webb, *The Making of a Navy Seal.* New York: St. Martin's Press, 2015. Print.
- Jocko Willink and Leif Babin, *Extreme Ownership.* New York: St. Martin's Press, 2015. Print.
- Malcolm Gladwell, *Outliers.* New York: Little, Brown, and Company, 2008. Print.
- Anders Ericsson and Robert Pool. *Peak: Secrets from the New Science of Expertise.* Boston: Houghton Mufflin Harcourt, 2016. Print.
- Angela Duckworth. *Grit.* New York: Scribner, 2016. Print.

Chapter 7
- Jennifer Hulett, Jane Armer, "A Systematic Review of Spiritually Based Interventions and

Psychoneuroimmunological Outcomes in Breast Cancer Survivorship."
https://journals.sagepub.com/doi/full/10.1177/153473
5416636222 Sage Journals. May 4, 2016. Web.

- Atul Gawande. *The Checklist Manifesto.* New York: Picador, 2009. Print.

- Carol Dweck. *Mindset.* New York: Penguin Random House, 2006. Print.

- Laurence Gonzales. *Deep Survival.* New York: W.W. Norton & Company, 2003. Print.

- Epictetus. *The Discourses.* (edited by Robert Dobbin). New York: Penguin Random House, 2008. Print.

Chapter 8

- John Ortberg. *If You Want to Walk on Water, You've Got to Get Out of the Boat.* Grand Rapids: Zondervan, 2001. Print.

- Robert Sanders. "Researchers find out why some stress is good for you".
https://news.berkeley.edu/2013/04/16/researchers-find-out-why-some-stress-is-good-for-you/. UC Berkeley. April 16, 2013. Web.

- Norman Garmezy, Ann Masten, Karin Best. "Resilience and development: Contributions from the study of children who overcome adversity".
https://www.cambridge.org/core/journals/developme nt-and-psychopathology/article/resilience-and-

developmet-contributions-from-the-study-of-children-who-overcome-adversity/9D84A6A2339F9B66E7B0B0D910F841CC. Cambridge University Press. October 1990. Web.

- Werner, E. E., & Smith, R. S. *Journeys from childhood to midlife: Risk, resilience, and recovery.* Ithaca, NY: Cornell University Press. 2001. Print.
- Laurence Gonzales. *Deep Survival.* New York: W.W. Norton & Company, 2003. Print.
- Malcolm Gladwell. *David and Goliath.* New York: Little, Brown and Company, 2013. Print.
- Jon Krakauer. *Into Thin Air.* New York: Anchor Books, 1997. Print.
- Beck Weathers. *Left for Dead.* New York: Bantam, 2000. Print.

Chapter 9

- Arash Javanbakht and Linda Saab. "What Happens in the Brain When We Feel Fear". Smithsonian Magazine. October 27, 2017: https://www.smithsonianmag.com/science-nature/what-happens-brain-feel-fear-180966992/. Web.
- Paul Whalen. "Human Amygdala Responsivity to Masked Fearful Eye Whites." Science 306. 2004.

- Greg Lukianoff and Jonathan Haidt. *The Coddling of the American Mind*. New York: Penguin Books, 2018. Print.
- Gary Hamel and C.K. Prahalad, *Competing for the Future*. Boston: Harvard Business School Press. 1994. Print.
- John Maxwell. *Failing Forward*. Nashville: Thomas Nelson Publishers, 2000. Print.
- Adam Grant. *Originals*. New York: Penguin Books, 2016. Print.
- Andy Grove. *Only the Paranoid Survive*. New York: Doubleday, 1999. Print.

Section III

- Allison Wood Brooks. "Get Excited: Reappraising Pre-Performance Anxiety as Excitement." Journal of Experimental Psychology: General 143. 2014.
- Jeff Haden. *The Motivation Myth*. New York: Penguin Books. 2018. Print.
- Richard Moore. *Mastermind: How Dave Brailsford Reinvented the Wheel*. Glasgow: BackPage Press. 2013. Print.
- Daniel Chambliss. "The Mundanity of Excellence: An Ethnographic Report on Stratification and Olympic Swimmers." Sociological Theory 7. 1989.

Chapter 10

- Norman Doidge, M.D.. *The Brain that Changes Itself.* London: Penguin Group, 2007. Print.
- David Goggins. "Can't Hurt Me". New York: Lioncrest Publishers. 2018. Print.
- Greg Lukianoff and Jonathan Haidt. *The Coddling of the American Mind.* New York: Penguin Books, 2018. Print.
- Malcolm Gladwell. *David and Goliath.* New York: Little, Brown and Company, 2013. Print.
- Amy Purdy. "On My Own Two Feet". New York: Harper Collins. 2014. Print.

Chapter 11

- G. Yue and K.J. Cole. "Strength increases from the motor program: Comparison of training with maximal voluntary and imagined muscle contradictions. Journal of Neurophysiology, 67 (5) 1992. Print.
- Norman Doidge, M.D.. *The Brain that Changes Itself.* London: Penguin Group, 2007. Print.
- Colin Cowherd. *You Herd Me.* New York: Crown Archetype, 2013. Print.

Made in the USA
Columbia, SC
16 May 2020